For my wife Barbara,

my junior in years, senior in wisdom

LAST LAUGHS

A Pocketful of Wry for the Aging

LAST LAUGHS

A Pocketful of Wry for the Aging

BY EVERETT MATTLIN

TWO HARBORS PRESS

Two Harbors Press
212 3rd Avenue North, Suite 290
Minneapolis, MN 55401
612.455.2293
www.TwoHarborsPress.com

ISBN-13: 978-1-936401-34-5
LCCN: 2011920955

Distributed by Itasca Books

Cover Design and Typeset by Elsa Angvall

Printed in the United States of America

WHO ARE THEY KIDDING?

●

Old age.

An elusive time zone, an indeterminate life passage.

Back when they started to keep track of such things, old age began at about 35—Methuselah excepted. Hit 50 and you were a phenomenon. But we've managed to stretch and stretch our mortal days until they're now talking about average life spans of 135, God forbid. Another fifty years of bingo games and Metamucil?

It's not easy these days to pinpoint when you are truly over the hill. Just where is that hill on life's map? Sixty? Certainly not. You're still rat-racing all over the place, as crazy and oblivious of mortality as ever. Seventy? Getting close. Seventy-five would seem about right. Will you agree that at seventy-five you deserve to stake your claim to old age, with all the rights and privileges thereto?

But I don't know. As I write this I've passed the eighty mark, and I seem to have a hard time convincing anyone that it's time to treat me with a little respect and deference.

"You're not old!" I'm assured, with a congratulatory laugh and a hearty slap on my arthritic back. "What can I do for you, young feller?" I'm asked by damn fools behind the counter, mocking any suggestion that I might be past my prime. People are living longer, which means I must have longer to live, never mind my having already lived a lifetime. Old age, it seems, keeps receding into a Neverland.

"Old" doesn't really exist, you see. It's a chimera, nothing but a mistaken state of mind, and we'd better change our minds if we suspect otherwise in this land that worships youth. Stop whining about your declining days and revel in your "power years."

Here's an ad featuring a man who marked his 100th birthday by waterskiing in Acapulco. And here's a story about a woman in her nineties who's begun working on her Ph.D. Another woman in her seventies confided to *Passages* author Gail

Sheehy that's she's finally found sexual bliss in the arms of a man in his eighties.

Where do they find these show-offs? And what are they trying to prove? I suspect even they must find their exertions more than slightly absurd. There was, and is, nothing wrong—in fact, everything right and proper—about old-style old age: the rocking chair, afternoon naps, sweet reminiscences over photo albums, re-watching favorite movies and rereading favorite books, quiet dinners with such friends as remain, staring into space and contemplating eternity. These should be our occupations and our pleasures, not physical and mental grandstanding. "Act your age" is good advice for more than growing children.

Indeed, one of the few positives about getting old should be the privilege of doing nothing, unless, of course, it's an activity you've always enjoyed and want to continue to enjoy as long as the ability's still there. You're not ready to roll over and play dead until it's no longer playing. But you have earned, by lasting this long, the inalienable right to pick the good stuff and toss the rest. The writer Anne Lamott says that she has finally learned that "'No' is a complete sentence."

You thought such freedom was the way it was going to

be after you retired, but you sabotaged yourself. You gathered a list of a million things you had been thinking about and planning and putting off during all your years of toil. Travel, volunteer work, the house, the garden, a new hobby, a family tree, photo albums, neglected reading, a language course—the list grew to absurd lengths. I seldom come across a recently retired person who doesn't say, "I seem busier than ever. I don't know where the day goes."

Ah, my friends, now the time has come when you just can't keep up that pace anymore. Your body balks at cooperating with your still compulsive will. If you've got any sense, you are relieved. Blessedly, a quiet and gentler time has arrived. Sloth is no longer a sin. It's a gift bestowed on survivors.

So don't listen to those sideline cheerleaders who would deny us our quiescence. They're a menace, oblivious to the facts of life's trajectory. Go to your Barnes and Noble and take a look at their duplicitous promises, books with titles and subtitles like *Stopping the Clock, Stop Aging Now, Life Beyond 100, Younger Next Year, The Six Steps to the Fountain of Youth, Healthy at 100, Add Ten Years to Your Life, Look Younger and Live Longer, The New Anti-Aging Revolution.* Bogus authorities would have us making love, making plans, making voyages, running marathons, climbing mountains, taking up yoga, learning to surf, motorcycling through the Dordogne, mastering Chinese and, for all I know, hunting wild boar on horseback with a bow and arrow in the Pakistani mountains.

And how are we to accomplish this annulment of nature's laws? The prescriptions in these books are a mixture of the common and the delusional. Exercise, of course. Smaller portions of "healthy" foods. Puzzles and puzzling games. Avoidance of stress, which seems to me impossible for the still living. An unwavering positive outlook no matter the depressing realities. To help matters along, make sure you get your daily intake of folic acid, manganese, potassium, selenium, zinc, iodine, calcium, thiamin, niacin, riboflavin, biotin, pantotheric acid, vitamins B to Z. And oh yes, I nearly forgot your fish-oil capsules. Put them all in a vat, stir, drink the magic elixir muttering the mantra "old age is a lie," and you can forget about dying.

And don't, whatever you do, eat a baked potato. Baked potatoes, says one guru, have a high glycemic index that "can damage cells and trigger inflammation." I love baked potatoes—yes, with sour cream and chives—and I've yet to wake up the next morning alarmingly inflamed.

The poppycock gets quantified. You've seen the quoted studies. "People with the highest intakes of beta-cryptoxanthin, an antioxidant . . . were about half as likely to develop inflammatory arthritis as those who get the least." The elderly "who did crossword puzzles four days a week had a risk of dementia 47 percent lower than subjects who did puzzles only once a week." Men who "bike for at least one hour a week enjoy a 29 percent lower mortality rate than sedentary men." Women "who ate chocolate once or twice a week lowered their risk of heart failure by 32%." "Gardening just one hour a week lowers risk of cardiac death by 66 percent." Does anyone really believe these snake-oil claims? Sixty minutes digging in the mud will plow the plaque out of your arteries?

I know what's going on. You can't pull the wool over these rheumy eyes. When society denies us our old age, it ignominiously weasels out of any responsibility for our welfare and comfort. I don't know about your experience, but it rarely occurs to anyone to offer me his or her seat on a bus the way proper folk were brought up to do when you and I were striplings. Young stalwarts watch with passive impatience as I struggle to get my suitcase in the plane's overhead bin. I'm still expected to rake the leaves and shovel the driveway. Oh, I get called "sir" now and then, and I get maybe 10 percent off at the Cineplex, and that's about it. Big deal.

So when, if ever, do we get to reap the rewards of having managed to keep breathing all these decades? When will others cede to our infirmities? I wait for the day when I can say, sorry, but I can't possibly help you with that weeding—my knees, you know. Sorry, but I get too tired at night to attend what I am sure will be a lovely party. Sorry, but I just can't manage babysitting my frisky granddaughters any more. Sorry, but I'm not up for long trips, so I won't be able to make it to your daughter's wedding in Omaha.

I'm beginning to think that day will never come. We're expected to keep up the same old pace, as though the multiplying years didn't matter. In our youth-obsessed society, those who can't are barely tolerated. Who needs stooped, wrinkled and blotched eyesores who can't even bicycle up Pike's Peak? Put 'em away in a pillared building with a long driveway and forget about 'em.

I've been thinking about moving to Japan. Over there— unless my information is dated—they still honor the elderly. And worship their ancestors. If I'm going to end up in a wheelchair, let the standing bow down.

Meanwhile, living in a country where old age is an embarrassment, I refuse to be conned into denial. I am old because I'm supposed to be old when I've lived this long. Who wants a perpetual frenetic youth anyway? I'll be damned if I'll spend my mornings in boring five-mile walks and my afternoons in health food stores.

You and I, we're mature in more than years. We accept the truth. We acknowledge our debilities and declining powers and have learned to live with them, sometimes stoically and sometimes with curses and tears. And with a wry laugh now and then. For there is much about old age, as about all of life, that is incongruous, and all you can do is laugh at the absurdity of it all. I hope there are some smiles in these pages. Maybe humor does more for a satisfying sunset than betacryptoxanthin.

GROUCHO LIVES

●

It's true, we old men are grumpy. Can't help ourselves. It comes with the prostatitis. Jack Lemmon and Walter Matthau dedicated the last years of their lives to educating the American public about this everlasting truth.

Not that old women are any different. Look, what do you expect? It's hard to be chirpy when your body keeps sending out sadistic bulletins. When what energy you have left after getting your socks on in the morning is used up preparing breakfast. When your mind does little but wander through the past, stopping at regrets. When your food is bland, or else. When your friends are dead, gaga, or unable to talk about anything but the progress of their deterioration. What is there, tell me, to sweeten one's disposition?

I know how sour mine is much of the time. I discover myself deplorably snappish. "You said my laundry would be ready at 4:00. Well, it's a quarter after, damn it, what have you done with it, lost it or sent it to China?" "I asked for my steak medium, not fresh from the abattoir." "I told you to leave off the whipped cream. My cholesterol will kill me soon enough, without your help." "Go away! I don't need you waving your arms, directing me into that parking spot. I was driving a car for a half century before you were born."

Well, I don't really say these things. But I think them.

I'm particularly short with service people in shops and over the phone because half the time I can't understand what the person I'm dealing with is saying. English is not a second language for these people; it's half a language. I know that it isn't very nice of me to be so intolerant. My father was an immigrant, after all, and his English wasn't exactly polished. But you could understand his every word. He moved to America, so he learned English, because that's what we speak here. Or used to. I don't see why so many announcements these days are repeated in Spanish. Spanish, as I understand it, is the language in Spain, and some other places. I repeat, I am a grump.

All right, I admit that I'm also peevish when I travel abroad and people, for some incomprehensible reason, don't understand English.

Some of this irascibility stems from simple impatience, because we oldsters know how precious time is. We have nothing particular to do, it's true, which would imply that we have all the time in the world, but we know we don't. Not in this world anyway. Only the young can thoughtlessly waste such a dwindling commodity. For children, only eternity exists. My granddaughter takes longer over a bowl of Fruit Loops than I do over dinner.

I grow grouchy when things go on too long. I seem to be in a hurry to go nowhere. When will this movie be over? Or this sermon? I won't read a book with more than 275 pages. Any delay sets me off. Traffic jams are personal affronts. I try to do my grocery shopping when there are no lines because everyone is doing something else, like watching the Super Bowl. Slow service at a restaurant ruins my meal. "Where the devil is that waiter? I haven't got all day." Who knows, I may not.

Homer Simpson's father once declared, "The good Lord lets us grow old for a reason: to gain the wisdom to find fault with everything He's made." And to deplore the botched "improvements" we humans ourselves have contributed. Who better than the old and experienced to recognize the shoddy and meretricious? We know a fool when we see one, and a phony. We are offended by a world that has failed to acquire our degree of discernment and reformed itself accordingly.

Not to be totally ostracized, we keep most of our dyspeptic judgments to ourselves. We just smile and nod politely. We swallow the words that come to mind, though they go down hard.

What a vicarious pleasure it is, therefore, when some old coot in a play—the movie version invariably tones down the vitriol--lets go with shocking candor. Like Big Daddy in *Cat on a Hot Tin Roof*, who calls his wife a "fat old body" and his grandchildren "five little monkeys." Or sour Norman Thayer in *On Golden Pond*, who tells his daughter's new boy friend, who's trying to be small-talk sociable, "Conversations bore me to tears," leaving the poor fellow speechless. Or the injured Sheridan Whiteside in *The Man Who Came to Dinner*, who tells his nurse that his great-aunt Jennifer "lived to be a hundred and two, and when she had been dead three days she looked better than you do now."

Outrageous, all of it. Never remotely excusable in real

life. But what fun to chortle over the vicious tongues of stage surrogates.

We old-timers sadly know, too, how much has deteriorated in our own lifetimes.

Take the matter of appropriate dress. We elders appreciate and honor decorum, a concept unknown to the young. It bugs me every time that in a fine restaurant--even at the opera--I am now practically the only man in the place under eighty wearing a tie. My wife likes the opera, so we're often there, but I grind my teeth in synch with the oboes when the guy sitting next to me in the magnificent Metropolitan Opera House is dressed for a picnic. I have to stop myself from turning to turn to him and saying, "Pardon me, sir, but I believe you've made a mistake, taken a wrong turn somehow and gotten lost. I'm afraid this is the opera house, not the race track." What's happened to respect for the grand occasion, the celebration of the special? I can't understand either how these slobs can afford the menu and ticket prices. Clearly, expensive doesn't keep out the people it once did.

Today's prices are troublingly disorienting for people my age. What you pay for a cup of coffee these days would have once bought a lunch. A meal at a posh restaurant would have paid for a decent suit. And what a suit from a place like Saks Fifth Avenue costs would have taken care of a week's vacation in Nassau. I understand inflation's compounding burden, but I still can't believe and won't accept these prices. They are clearly outrageous. I may pay up, let them rob me, but not without the grumbling resentment of the fleeced.

Aside from the prices, restaurant menus have become ridiculous. Unless you eat at a diner, you can't understand what they intend to feed you. The first entrée offering at a place in my neighborhood that calls itself "An American Bistro" is "escabeche of sea scallops, banyuls reduction, garlic coulis." I am forever asking my wife the meaning of coulis, confit, rillette, salsify, ramps, crostini, comichon, wasabi, aioli, soubise, timbale, tabouleh, tapenade, pancetta, frisse, relleno, and other such ubiquitous obscurities. Of course I immediately forget the definition, and annoy her by asking the same questions the next night out.

A review of Manhattan's posh Jean Georges restaurant raved that "a seared baby chicken, served without bones and crowned with a crunchy crust of seven different breakfast cereals, is only $19." What a bargain! And I'll have, let's see, Rice Crispies, Captain Crunch, Cinnamon Life. . . . The fashionable has become risible.

Another dining innovation that bugs me: when did the routine start of the waiter, head-waiter, maître d, chef and for all I know the owner coming around at every course, or twice every course, asking, "How is everything? Okay?" Their continuous need for reassurance--an irritating interruption of food and talk--tempts me to reply, "No, the food is not okay. It's awful, a disgrace at any price, much less yours. But I'm eating it, aren't I, so just go away."

And why this craze for Thai, Indian, Sushi, Greek, Ethiopian and other alien cuisines? I still value "good home cooking," and my mother never served such stuff in my house.

I'm not done with the subject of male clothing either. If I wore those "designer" outfits (when did tailors get upgraded to designer status?) that I see in magazine ads—you know the ones I mean, the Armani and Hugo Boss suits modeled by surly, dissolute young dropouts in need of a shave, a haircut or at least a comb, and probably a good kick in the pants—I'd feel I had dressed for a costume ball. Columnist Maureen Dowd says that where she came from any man who wore such clothes would be dismissed as a gigolo. I'll stick to good old Brooks Brothers, though even the Brothers have gone a trifle too faddish for my tastes. And while on the subject, when did spread-collar business shirts take over from button-downs and straight collars? For older men like me, with jowls and wattled necks, a spread collar makes it looks as though the shirt had a regular collar until we put it on and squashed it. As for those shirts with colored or striped bodies and white collars and cuffs, I consider them fit only for clerks in London banks and ambassadors from third-world countries.

Our complaints aren't just nostalgia for an imagined past. Many things *were* better back then, however you care to define "back then." It was much more sensible, for example, when hotels gave you a key to your room, with the room number clearly engraved on it. Now they hand you a numberless piece of plastic. I would wander the halls in perpetuity if I didn't write my room number down and carry the slip of paper around with me the duration of my stay. I don't know about you, but the plastic card takes me an average of three attempts to get it to work. Sometimes it doesn't, and I have to go down to the lobby and wait in line to get a new one. Keys always worked.

Something else bugs me, though it doesn't seem to disturb the rest of mankind in the slightest. When did people stop saying "good-bye" or "thank you" and start with this "Have a nice day" sign-off? By the fifth iteration of the day I vow I will throttle the next person that says that to me. The clerk who hands me my receipt with a "Have a good one" seems to think himself the cleverest fellow in the world for this riff on the usual. "Have a great day" is the stupidest of all. How many great days have I had in my whole lifetime?

The historian and critic Paul Fussell relishes the response of a British friend when he hears "Have a nice day." He smiles and says, "Thank you, but I have other plans."

We curmudgeons are needed to correct the follies of the world, for as Jon Winokur has explained, we "refuse to see life through the filter of wishful thinking and are outspoken in our devotion to the harsh realities of life." It's not a pleasant job, but we undertake it for the good of all.

I am not ungrateful for the conveniences of progress during my lifetime. I appreciate the microwave that makes my lunch, the videos that allow me to watch Fred Astaire dance to my heart's content, the cell phone that allows me to call from my car to announce that I'm "running late but on my way," when I've only just left the garage. (Though I make calls on the cell phone, I hardly ever receive them, because I never remember to turn the thing on until I need to make a call. This drives my wife crazy, since she can't reach me to let me know that the doctor's nurse just called to cancel the appointment I am rushing to keep.)

I particularly cherish the appliance to end all appliances, my computer, the beloved companion of my old age. I don't understand a quarter of the machine's powers, but that doesn't matter. We play many games together, whiling away endless carefree hours. Still, I get very short-tempered with my friend. I do something wrong—hit some peripheral key, I suppose--and the screen startles me with unintelligible hieroglyphics, or delivers some dire message, like "This program has performed an illegal operation and you are under immediate house arrest." Every other week I have to call my engineer son in Pasadena to ask what I should do to correct a problem so I can go back to my game of solitaire.

"Are there no joys left in your life?" you ask, appalled that I don't appreciate the gift of every breath left me. Of course there are. The sight of a patrol car nabbing a driver recklessly weaving in and out of traffic. The election defeat of some pandering, air-headed politician. A public pietist arrested for sexual misconduct. Obituary-page days when all the newly deceased failed to reach my present age.

Yes, indeed, however burdensome life has become, it still manages to offer its little smiles of satisfaction.

CAN WE GO HOME NOW?

●

You've finally reached the age of retirement, eager to begin all that traveling you've so long and hungrily contemplated. Not Bryce Canyon or the Canadian Rockies or Alaska or Tuscany—you've done all those. Now's the moment for Bangkok, the Galapagos, Petra, Botswana, Agra, Machu Picchu, the distant, the exotic, the tantalizing.

My advice is to do it now, quick, all of it, get it out of your system. Because before too long, you won't want to go anywhere where a car can't take you in under half an hour.

It's always been a hassle to get ready for a long trip, the stopping the mail and newspaper, getting the dog to the kennel, finding someone to check on the house to make sure it hasn't "burned to the ground," as my mother invariably predicted, buying the travel-size toothpaste and deodorant, agonizing over what clothes to take in what suitcases. But the stress intensifies with each passing birthday.

You get to the age when you check your travel schedule twice a day for weeks, you plan and re-plan and re-re-plan what to pack, you sleep poorly for five nights before departure, you are convinced you have forgotten to take care of something vital or pack something essential, like your heart medication. You are leaving the familiar security of home for the unknown, and the anxiety is wearing you down before you've even left your house.

Plagued by the thought that you'll miss your flight because of an accident on the expressway, you get to the airport three hours early. You'd really feel better if you'd gotten there the night before, maybe slept in a tent in the waiting area.

Airports have become a gauntlet for everyone, as we all know. For older people it's cruel punishment. You wait in long lines, like a bereft supplicant, first for check-in—there are now machines you can use, but machines are for the young—and then security, until your legs and back ache and your once light carry-on has mysteriously put on surprising weight. For the security check, you undress, like in the doctor's office, including your shoes, which are hell to get back on. You forget to take the Rolaids out of your pocket, whose foil sets off the beeper, forcing the prod and pat-down, which makes you feel a fool. And angry: how could a weak wreck like you threaten national security?

If you've been rolling a suitcase behind you—your right shoulder and neck also signal trouble—lifting it onto the rollers for X-raying requires a small prayer. (Forget about getting it into an overhead bin; you look desperately for a young face, one with a trace of kindness instead of the usual vacuity.)

Walks to and from gates seem to get longer and longer as terminals expand their acreage. A half-mile is about the median. You now wish you'd rented one of those luggage carts, not just to hold your bags but for something to lean on during your pilgrimage, but you hate laying out $3 for what should be a free courtesy, especially to the feeble. And you're not going to be pushed along the corridors in a wheelchair. Not yet, damn it.

Finally you are at the gate, relieved to sit down. Quiet would be nice, too, but the television screens are blaring above you no matter where you sit. You still have an hour and a half before boarding time, and then they announce that the departure will be delayed for twenty minutes. It ends up forty. If you're really unlucky, there's a gate change, and it's more schlepping. Half a day has gone by, and you are tired and irritable, wondering if this whole trip was such a good idea.

Finally, you sink in your appointed seat (you requested an isle, ready egress to the bathrooms). After interminable hours, indifferent food, a childish movie, you arrive. If it's been a night flight, you managed to sleep two hours, if that—which class you're in doesn't matter--and you are dead tired and your back is killing you. If you had any sense, you booked a tour, so someone else is battling with luggage, currency exchange, transport to the hotel, and that most irksome business, tipping.

Young bodies can tolerate long flights, changes in time zones and radical disruptions in routine. The set-in-their-ways have lost adaptability. Foreign beds are either too hard or too soft, the showers a bad joke, the toilet paper more like tissue paper. You've been told not to drink the tap water but forget when taking your nightly quota of pills, and wonder what microbes you'll be importing. You soon find that Metamucil can't figure out how to interact with alien cuisines, and several days of constipation are followed by a bout of diarrhea. Health in general is a constant nag. What if your intestinal bleeding acts up and you have to be operated on in a Phnom Penh hospital?

You're there to see the sights, but the seeing is exhausting. You aren't used to walking for hours, much less climbing steps to imperial palaces and scrambling over stones at crumbling ruins. You're short of breath and a little dizzy from the exertion, and a higher altitude doesn't help. One attraction men are always on the lookout for is a bathroom. Women mysteriously manage to refrain until back at the hotel's well-scrubbed facilities.

Much that you see fascinates, whether it be giant turtles, Hindu shrines or simply street life in an alien culture. But you are soon admitting to yourself that you're not as caught up in it all as you would have been when younger. The desire to learn, to absorb the new, has ebbed. You find your mind wandering during the guide's spiel and wishing she'd cut it short. Today's Buddhist temple looks very much like the one you saw yesterday and the day before that, and after the third sighted whale, the thrill is muted. You are disoriented and wearied by too much unfamiliarity. It would be nice to be back at the hotel with a cup of tea and a paperback. A nap would be even better. A nap in your good old bed back home, come to think of it, would be delicious.

No wonder cruises are so popular with the elderly. No

language or currency concerns. Familiar food. Recognizable faces. Care and comfort always at hand. You are traveling, but bringing most of your known world with you.

Cruises arrange shore treks, of course, and you're sure to sign up, for why else come all this distance if not to marvel at the marvels? The rewards of glacier and castle can live up to expectations, but getting to the sites is often a long drag, for you are at the mercy of a garrulous guide with a microphone and a captive audience. Whether he is told that paying guests must be entertained or he fancies himself an adjunct to show biz, he never shuts up. After a few lame jokes, his narrative goes something like this:

"On the right you see the Bondinanny Bridge, over the Krakousti River, which is 576 meters deep, the deepest river in the region. The bridge was started in 1969 and built in eighteen months and three days at a cost of approximately two and a half million zlotys. A tunnel was considered but the idea was abandoned. A ferry service was considered but the idea was abandoned. If there were no bridge, cars and trucks would have to drive 77.5 kilometers to the bridge at Trikoistok. The toll to cross the Bondinanny is 10 zlotys per car, plus 2 zlotys per passenger.

When the bridge is paid for, in another estimated 43 years, the toll will be lifted.

"On your left now is a fine example of a local farmhouse. On your right is a fine example of a local church. Walking on the path ahead of us is a fine example of a local. The pine forest you now see on both sides supplied the timber for both the farmhouse and the church.

"We are now entering the town of Gudvangen, population 4,026. The town was founded in 1264 and was completely destroyed by fire in 1265. It was rebuilt in 2003, which explains why a medieval village looks so new. On your left is the just completed city hall. The old city hall is now used to store fish. Notice the stonework over the doorway—sardines, the local staple. To the left are stores and to the right are stores; these are where the inhabitants shop. We are now passing, on the right, the Kluminka key chain factory, the only local industry. The statue in front is Rudolph Kluminka, its founder and town benefactor—he donated money for the benches in the park on your left. This afternoon, on our return, we'll stop here and you can you see how key chains are made and buy souvenirs and gifts to take back home."

When you are indeed blessedly back home, you assure all

who politely inquire that it was a marvelous trip, full of wonders, and show them the pictures to prove it. To yourself you vow, "Okay, yes, but probably enough. I think it's time to store the magic carpet in the attic."

When Vanity Fair asked Sue Mengers, identified as a "Hollywood super agent," to name her favorite journey, she replied, "From the living room to the bedroom." Unexpectedly sensible from a super agent.

I know there are admirable exceptions, travelers, even in their eighties, who are ever-alert, receptive, eager and indefatigable. Bless them all. May they traverse the globe in never-ending astonishment. Me, I'll rent National Geographic videos.

DUMBBELLS ARE FOR DUMBBELLS

•

Here it is, in pontifical print: "You're never too old to exercise, and you're never so old that you shouldn't."

I swear, the day you're dying they'll bring a barbell to your bed and ask you to do a few bench presses before they pull the sheet over you.

Why can't they leave us alone, to grow old and feeble and dependent the way God and nature intended? My mother lived to 92, and I assure you that it was without benefit of a personal trainer.

But dammit, you shout in my ear, we *do* need exercise, no matter how old we are. Of course we do. And we get it—when we walk the dog, clean up after the dog, play with the grandchildren, clean up after the grandchildren, go down the stairs with the laundry, go up the stairs with the laundry, walk from the parking lot to the grocery store, shop for the groceries, walk back to the parking lot, go for the newspaper, go for the mail, go to the refrigerator, go to the sink, go to bed. As Nora Ephron has explained, "exercise" is a modern invention. People always did it, but didn't think of it as exercise. "They thought of it as life itself." Exactly! Our bodies are up to something all the time, so why this crazy exhortation to punish them with superfluous exertion?

To be honest, I've never been much of an exercise fan, even when young and passably able. I'm with Henry Ford, who called exercise "bunk." He explained that "if you are healthy, you don't need it, and if you are sick, you shouldn't take it." Ford almost made it to 84, which isn't too bad, considering the time he spent around car exhausts.

Mark Twain reached his mid-seventies without relaxing his lifelong disparagement of exercise. "It cannot be any benefit when you are tired," he said, "and I was always tired." And don't tell me that exercise would have energized the crusty old fellow. If you aren't more tired after exercise than you were before you started, you've been up to nothing that deserves the name.

The very word "exercise" bothers me.

It's the "ex" that does it, I think, the "from," taking from, as in excavate, exorcise, exhume, expunge, exclude, expectorate, excommunicate, not to mention extinct, exhaust and expire. We instinctively sense that the truth behind all the propaganda is that exercise doesn't add anything to your life, it extracts from it.

Advocates of a run, jump, flex and lift regimen argue that we have become such sedentary people—bound to our desks instead of threshing wheat, driving our cars instead of walking five miles to church, riding in a golf cart instead of traipsing under a 90° sun--that we need injections of vigorous movement. That's the common wisdom. How about the common sense? Think what a strain it is to the system when someone accustomed to full days in a lounging posture abruptly starts jumping around on a court or running along a path like prehistoric man fleeing a mastodon. It stands to reason that this irregular spasmodic behavior is a shock and insult to the heart, lungs and every other vital organ. No wonder we so often hear of deaths on the jogging trail or handball court. (I confess that I greet such reports with a smug smile.)

Ah, you object, but of course one must exercise in moderation. Too much, by definition, is excessive, and therefore dangerous. But what does your doctor caution you about alcohol? "A drink or two before dinner won't hurt you." The implication is clear: while modest intake tempers the risk, none at all would be risk-free. The same logic applies to exercise. "Don't overdo it now!" The safest thing would be not to do it at all.

Most people detest exercise as much as I do, however much they deny it to justify what they laid out for a lifetime gym membership. Why else the diversionary television sets placed in front of every treadmill, stationary bike and stair-stepper and the headsets haloed around almost every runner? We have to anesthetize our minds against our aversion to the tedium of the thing. When we force ourselves to do that which the mind abhors--well, you know what the psyche can do to the soma.

The constant body evaluation that comes with the routine adds another insidious element. The apprehensive trips to the scale, the appraisals in the mirror, the subjecting of oneself to continual critical once-overs that lead to continual disappointments, for bodily perfection ended with the Greeks. The whole process is masochistic from beginning to end.

Exercise helps you lose weight? Come on now. You know,

by sad experience, that it's not true. A half hour on a treadmill at the pace that people our age can manage uses up a hundred calories or so, which is meaningless. Worse still, it builds an appetite for "a little something" that repays the hundred and then some. When dinner comes, we help ourselves to an extra sliver of pie as a justified reward for the infernal sweat session. It's the same syndrome that sends me to Ben and Jerry's after a stint in the dentist's chair.

If you're dead set on doing *something* to feel virtuous, I suggest exercise lite--billiards, perhaps, or shuffleboard. Even swimming, if it doesn't turn into one of those lap-flip-lap, lap-flip-lap, lap-flip-lap endurance tests. Golf leads to skin cancers and too much drinking in the clubhouse. Tennis is okay, if it's doubles with people as feeble as you are. The goal is recreation and enjoyment, which has nothing to do with exercise.

Trust me, you'll be just fine without suffering all that grunt-and-groan nonsense. Don't listen to those sententious doctors. Chances are they never go near a gym. Probably overweight, too. Smokers on the sly?

LESS IS BEST, MORE OR LESS

●

The wise men in white smocks tell us that to thwart heart attacks, strokes, diabetes, back pain and, for all I know, scalp itch, we need to stay thin. Well, thin would be asking too much. Say, somewhat thin. I don't know about you, but in my case, that means losing weight. A good deal of weight, if you really insist upon knowing.

But hell, I haven't had a heart attack yet, or a stroke, or diabetes—knock on wood three times—and my luck may hold out. Besides, these fries are the best in town.

I don't know who said it, but I'll bet he was Italian: "The true philosophy is to grow plump." As far as I am concerned, he was a Solomon.

I had an aunt who used to say, mostly just after looking in

bakery windows, "If the Good Lord didn't want us to eat cakes and pies and all that, He wouldn't have made them so delicious." Praise the Lord and pass the cannoli.

No, what has finally convinced me to pare down is not so much health as aesthetics. The sight of so many men and women my age, and far younger, who have gone to pot--their bellies over-flowing—has disturbed my complacency. I wear fulsome shirts whose camouflaging drapery may fool others, but I can't kid myself. A look in the full-length mirror after showering provides all the prima facie evidence needed to convict. Front-on doesn't look too bad. But in profile, ugh! Those curvatures, fore and aft, are anything but sexy. Disgusting is more like it. M'god, I look like *them*. Something must be done.

"Eat less" is the obvious solution. I had another aunt whose admonition was "always leave something on your plate." Given Aunt Hilda's cooking, that was easy. But when my plate is filled with my wife's divine dishes (what else could I put into print?), I can't stop. And even when the food in a restaurant is only so-so, surely you can't expect me to leave food behind. Not at these prices.

Besides, "eat less" lacks precision. If I'm going to get serious about downsizing, I'll need a discipline. I'll never get there without a map. Otherwise known as a diet.

Have you perused the shelves of diet books at Border's of late? A salmagundi of choices. Shall it be the Dr. Atkins, the South Beach, the Mediterranean, the Glycermic Index, the Sonoma, the Hollywood or some other strappado? Here's one called *The New Cabbage Soup Diet*. I loathe cabbage. I suppose if I ate only cabbage soup for weeks on end I'd have the body I had when a sophomore in high school, but it would be lying in a coffin.

To tell you the truth, I can't stomach any diets. I haven't the patience for tables that spell out the grams of harm in every conceivable food, for keeping a diary of each morsel of intake, for measuring out the three-and-a-half ounces of chicken, the half cup of mushrooms, the tablespoon of onions, the third of a red pepper, the thin slice of bread and the teaspoon of margarine that will coalesce as dinner. I have no use for a recipe for artichoke and spinach soup. I can't imagine dining on 1 ½ cups of Soba noodles, whatever they are, in peanut sauce. I do not consider five unsalted mini rice cakes a snack worth snacking on. A half cup of fat-free, sugar-free pudding made with fat-free milk doesn't deserve to be called dessert.

Ah, dessert! All the diets are so prejudiced against them. Whenever we dine out with friends, my wife annoyingly enjoys telling the others that her husband reads the menu from the bottom up. Well, yes, as a matter of fact I do. You have to eat the other stuff first, I know, and some of it can be quite good, but what really matters is the denouement. It's like a fireworks display--all glorious, but with the best blast saved for last.

So you really can't ask me to give up Häagen-Dazs vanilla and Ben & Jerry's Phish Food and lemon meringue pie and strawberry shortcake and Mars bars and hot fudge sundaes and oatmeal raisin cookies and napoleons and tiramisu and peach cobbler and crème brulée and seven-layer cake and . . . well, I'll stop, though just the recitation itself brings inner joy. If I gave them all up, I'd probably be thin. And surely be miserable. On those rare occasions when I've denied myself my usual "little something," to quote Piglet, a half hour later I am in a sweat and head for the freezer trough for a fix. Should I go cold turkey on desserts, the withdrawal trauma would be terrible to contemplate. I want my heirs to sue any doctor who advises it.

I've made one concession, however. With lapses, I've

substituted frozen yoghurt for ice cream. The yoghurt has fewer calories, and you can eat as much of it as you like. At least I am making that assumption, since I've always been told that yoghurt is good for you, that tribesmen in Kazakhstan or someplace like that who eat little else live to an average age of 106. I also know that regular yoghurt must be good for you because it tastes so bad, so off-puttingly sour no matter what berries they bury in its depths. But when they freeze the stuff instead of leaving it molten, it tastes good. Proof again of the saving grace of sugar.

I don't know why sugar should be such an anathema to the Drs. Atkins, Pritikin, Ornish and the rest of the admonitory pack. After all, it's cholesterol-free and a natural food, all the craze these days.

Tell me, please, now that the subject has been raised, when did all this nonsense about natural and organic food start? For most of my life, anyway, the word "organic" had something to do with chemistry and nothing to do with food. And we got along just fine without all the fuss.

Now we have organic apples, carrots, potatoes, bread, pasta, pasta sauce, crackers, corn flakes, milk, butter, yoghurt, popcorn, lemonade, tomato juice, sausages, pancake syrup, cookies, jelly, cake mixes and peanut butter—not to mention dog and cat food and "natural" napkins and paper towels. It's ridiculous, a craze like feng shui, which dictates the spiritual placement of your living room sofa. I think people who shop organic just want to feel virtuous, like environmentalists, vegetarians, antivivisectionists and spotted owl preservers. You're not going to sucker me into driving crosstown for a virginal head of lettuce or unpolluted corn chips.

To lose one pound, the experts say, you need to reduce your food-and-drink intake by 3,500 calories. That's about ten hearty desserts. In a month, if I foreswear my goodies, I will lose three pounds. In a year, even with a bit of cheating, I could take off thirty pounds. Now that is impressive.

But wait. If I also gave up wine and beer and the harder stuff, I would subtract roughly the same number of calories from my current non-diet diet. So if I abandoned both desserts *and* alcohol, I could lose sixty pounds in a year.

In not much over three years I'd weigh nothing.

Something's wrong here. The experts clearly don't know what they're talking about. One would be a fool to follow the advice of such muddleheads. I'd best stick with both the desserts and the wine until they get their story straight.

Meanwhile, I haven't solved my problem. I must make some sacrifice if I am to progress in slimming my silhouette. I must give up *something*.

How about vegetables?

WHA'DJA SAY?

●

I've owned a pair of hearing aids for at least seven years. Occasionally, I even wear them.

I've yet in my travels among the elderly to find a soul who doesn't profess a troubled relationship with his or her hearing assists. They distort, they amplify background noise to the prejudice of the person sitting next to you, they in general irritate. "It's because you don't wear them all the time," chastised the purveyor of my little amoeba-shaped pair. "You'll love them once you get used to them." What else could she say, after depositing my $4,000?

My insurance company is deaf to pleas of reimbursement. Apparently the inability to hear is less important than a sore throat.

Though most aids owners I know are now-and-then users like myself, I also know one exception, a man never ear-naked. But he is one decibel away from totally deaf. I have to shout at him in spite of his auxiliary amplification system. Without it, he would know nothing at all of the world's music and laughter.

I've wondered about that $4,000 price tag. Why all that money for pieces of plastic no bigger than the kidney beans they resemble? A formidable Buck-Rogers-design remote-controlled Panasonic sound system, with AM/FM tuner (when did they stop calling them radios?), cassette and multiple-disk CD player and three-way speakers (with 6 ½ woofers, whatever they are) can be had at Best Buy for under $150. My wife's Blackberry, which fits easily within her dainty hand, delivers E-mail and the Internet, displays photographs, offers music and video, plays games with her, and stores her date calendar, address book, all manner of files and documents and, for all I know, the Encyclopedia Britannica and the Oxford English Dictionary, and it retails for less than $500. But there are many such economic mysteries the consumer is clearly forbidden to unravel.

Forgetting the cost, the plugs are indeed difficult to befriend. I suppose I am indeed to blame for my discomfiture, since

I so seldom wear them. When they are uncharacteristically in place, a pie tin dropped on the tile kitchen floor sounds like the firing on Fort Sumter, and when I urinate I am reminded of the poet Southey's cataract at Lodore.

I keep trying to employ them in restaurants, especially when more than four of us are at table, believing it would be pleasant—and polite—to hear what everyone has to say. I am soon disabused of that hope and take the damn things out, for whatever my companions offer is drowned out by babble from other tables and the clatter of plates, silver and glassware until I feel like we're dining near a battlefield. So I sit there, laughing at jokes I haven't heard and nodding agreement to assertions un-communicated.

I understand that newer models are more user-friendly, but a hike in price naturally accompanies the improvements. Anyway, what would I do, throw the old $4,000 pair in the wastebasket? Is it really worth all that money to allow me to hear things that, for the most part, are inconsequential to my well-being? In any case, am I really all that deaf? My friends don't tell me my hearing is worse, because they are friends. My wife and children can be forthright about my fading powers, but if family can't put up with some louder repetitions, what good are they?

The one occasion when I do make sure I have the little devils in place is at the theater (movies usually blast loudly enough), so that I won't have to *sotto voce* my wife every five minutes about what critical piece of dialog I have just missed. The earphones provided gratis at most theaters these days are probably more efficient, but when the curtain falls, I like to leap out of my seat and sprint down the aisle in order to win the race to the garage and be first out of the place. My game is blown if I have to return earphones to retrieve my driver's license.

My hearing aids work well enough in auditoriums, except for those times when half way through the first act I'm aware of static developing in one ear and know the battery needs replacing. If I'm lucky, I've remembered to bring spares. Fumbling to change a battery, by feel in the dark, making squeaking noises that infuriate my neighbors, is a skill I haven't quite mastered. I either drop the hearing aid and grope around under my seat, further disturbing those around me, or the replacement battery slips away and bounces into obscurity. I've spent many an intermission on a theater's floor searching for a $2,000 blob of plastic.

Of course, if it's a Broadway musical I'm attending, I

don't need hearing aids. Even my near-deaf friend would catch every last note. The amplification these days is such that what I now need in my ears is cotton wool.

I also wear the aids at home when we watch television, and they do their job, unless we're watching Masterpiece Theatre or Mystery or some other BBC production. For some reason—and others of the elderly have confirmed this puzzling phenomenon--I cannot understand the half of what British actors are saying, especially the female ones. With some Austen or Trollope adaptation, it doesn't matter much, because I can pretty much figure out what's going on. But the mysteries leave me mystified. I lose out on vital clues and motives and the fine points of the inevitable recapitulation of the case between the preternaturally perceptive detective and his cipher sidekick. To be honest, even if I could hear it all clearly it wouldn't matter much, because I am no longer able to remember the names of the characters—a.k.a. suspects—so whenever such critical information as the whereabouts of those under suspicion at the time of the crime is reviewed, I haven't the faintest idea whom they're talking about.

My wife pleads with me to wear my aids all the time. She, most understandably, wearies of my response of "Sorry, dear, what did you say?" to nine-tenths of her utterances. More vexing are the many times I don't hear what she's said but make an educated guess—that is, a stab in the dark—about her likely comment or query. I'm only trying to avoid another "Sorry, dear," etc. and suffering her irritation, but I almost always make things worse. "No, I didn't ask you if you've taken out the trash. I wanted to know if you want me to save the leftovers for hash."

I can swear at my hearing aids and boycott them, but in the end I know they'll triumph. I can't exactly expect my hearing to improve. Ere long I'll be like my quasi-deaf friend, grateful for any help in hearing at least some of what the world has to tell me. How can I contradict everyone if I don't know what they're saying?

SECOND-BEST BED

●

Some time ago my wife banished me from our bed. Now, her bed.

My masculine amour-propre took a hit, but I'd been expecting the dismissal. My snoring has become ever more stentorious as the years roll on, confirmed by the entire household at breakfast when I stay over at my son's house in New Jersey. Arthritis and sciatica keep me thrashing, searching for comfort. My unruly prostate sends me to the bathroom several times a night, the little pills notwithstanding. And another offense, indelicate to specify, involves my wayward digestive tract.

All in all, I could hardly blame my wife for wanting to get me out of there so she can enjoy an undisturbed night's sleep. Her martyrdom deserved closure.

At first I fussed over this abrogation of the marriage contract, but it wasn't long before I realized the advantages of the new arrangement.

I can now snore the Anvil Chorus and make other old-man noises without consequence. I can stretch and squirm and roll over and over to my body's content.

I sleep in greater comfort since leaving the matrimonial bed. My wife prefers few blankets, I like a pile-up. Now she can diminish while I augment. She likes a hard mattress, and I had never adjusted to sleeping on stone. I bought myself a cushy job and sink into sleep with a sigh and a smile.

Equally significant, I have my own room, territorially staked-out. I am master of my own domain, a replica of bachelorhood. If I don't make the bed in the morning, so what? No one is going to change my carpets, drapes, bedspread and wallpaper every three years. Come to think of it, I don't even know if the walls are papered or painted, and I don't care enough to go upstairs and check.

I no longer have to open my wardrobe drawers in secret, to avoid my wife's passing by and tut-tutting about the anarchy within. Ditto my chaotic closet. I like disarray. It bespeaks a freedom of spirit, a manly disregard for petty fussiness, a snub to stultifying formality.

Vacations are still a problem. On occasion, in the boonies somewhere, we've been able to take two $89-a-night rooms to enjoy separate but equal facilities. When our son was younger and not yet embarrassed to vacation with his parents, I often found myself sharing a room with him, leaving my spouse to peaceful slumber. Children should be willing—nay, eager--to suffer for the comfort of their parents, don't you agree?

When unavoidably sharing a hotel room or cruise cabin, my wife and I always request twin beds, but my invariable nocturnal melodies carry far. Often, too, scrambling in the dark to find my Mylanta tablets or the little flashlight I pack to light my way to the toilet, I drop something or make enough night-table noise that I hear movement from the other bed. In the morning, I don't have to ask. My wife's tired eyes and grim silence tell all.

If our vacation is spent at the beach, we rent a house. She sleeps in Bedroom A and I in Bedroom B. You can find me just over there, on the other side of the place, one floor down.

All considered, our various living arrangements have proved quite satisfactory to both parties, and nuptial vows have been renewed for an indefinite term. We each rule a domain, negotiating amicably about such matters as ownership of our plumpest pillows and the temperature setting for the floor where we both lay our heads.

Ah, but I can tell you have been thinking about something else. You've been wondering, about this separate-beds compact. The eternal prurient, eh? Well, it's none of your business. My wife and I still share the same house, after all. Besides, consider my age and let the matter drop.

IT'S A PUZZLEMENT

•

Alzheimer's—that nasty black cloud that hovers over our declining years.

How we all dread it, pray that it passes our door. We've seen how it turns people into non-people. We shiver at the thought of becoming a body without the soul we've just spent a lifetime honing. If there's to be a resurrection of the dead, as religion tells us, they'll have a lot of preparatory rewiring to do on the other side.

With rare exceptions, we all suffer some degree of memory loss as we age, and that's probably not a bad thing. Disappointments and regrets better forgotten conveniently slip the mind. Impaired memory may be nature's way of helping us gradually let go of that which was our life. If life, as they say, is a dream, let it become as hazy as most of our dreams. When the time comes to depart this world, we'll be giving up what we can no longer distinctly recall.

Fear of dementia strikes even the young. How often I hear striplings in their thirties say, when they can't think of the name of a distant cousin or have forgotten where they left their car keys, "My memory's not what it used to be." This confession is accompanied by a sad shake of the head, as though senility were waiting just around the next birthday.

The wise men in white coats advise us to stave off, or at least mollify, Alzheimer's, by exercising the mind. Keep the computer up there humming. Master Arabic, take up calculus, read Wittgenstein, decipher the da Vinci code. The recommendation that tops most lists I've seen is crossword puzzles.

Fine. Crosswords involve no travel and minimal expense. But there are problems.

First of all, there are so many answers that not even Ken Jennings would know, like the name of a city in Kyrgystan (Osh) or the composer of "Mercure" (Satie) or the first name of the Polish poet Mickiewicz (Adam). What, you don't know the name of the lead role in Rimsky-Korsakov's "The Maid of Pskov"?

It's Ivan, you ignoramus. The obscurities that puzzle composers dredge up out of some buried computer file irritate me. I feel I'm being asked to know what no one else on earth knows, that the author is taunting me, laughing at having lured me into a cul de sac. Old people don't need such aggravation.

Even when the answers to clues aren't obscure to the general populace, they're mysteries to us oldsters. How am I supposed to know who created the comic strip Hagar the Horrible? Or the star of some TV series called "Barbershop?" Or the last names of movie stars whose unlikely first names are Orlando, Joaquin, Charlize, Topher, Heath and Kyra? (When did Hollywood decide that Jimmy and Kate and Fred aren't good enough? I have to admit, though, that Humphrey was a rather odd moniker. Sort of a clinker, ha, ha.) Or the name of the "rapper" who had a hit called "Body Rock"? Or who hip-hop's Kanye West is? I don't even know what hip-hip is, and have no intention of researching the topic.

Ah, you protest, but there is a compensatory advantage to being old. We know the stuff that's a blank to the 35-year-old. We know who Sammy Kaye and Enos Slaughter and Preston Sturges and Walter Winchell and John Nance Garner and Nelson

Eddy and Ida Lupino and Rosa Ponselle and Admiral Nimitz and Mammy Yokum are, or were.

But there's a catch. A maddening catch. Yes, we know these things, but we can't for the like of us remember their names when it comes time to fill in the blanks. She won an Oscar for *Come Back, Little Sheba*, yes, yes, she was terrific, but her name, her name, damn it. "Hon, do you remember who starred in *Sheba*? She played opposite, oh, blast it, I can't think of his name either."

Crosswords may be a greater danger than the one they are supposed to prevent. I'm sure frustration over elusive facts and names stokes my blood pressure to perilous heights.

I'll tell you how I've solved the problem. I skip the puzzles in the newspapers (easy Mondays excepted) and buy books of puzzles with the answers in back. When an answer is on the tip of my memory but not quite captured, or I'm asked a stupid question—like the currency in Djibouti—I look up the answer and go on from there. I've become quite adept at selective peeping. At least it keeps me sane for now. You may think me an intellectual wimp, but I don't mind. I'll live on, my marbles intact.

By the way, what do marbles have to do with anything, anyway?

NO, NO, NARCISSUS

●

Mirrors make one reflect.

My own visual tête-à-têtes with my mirrored self always begin with surprise. What stares back at me is never quite what I expect. That has to be me, of course. It's doubtless what others see. Still, yet again, the mirror's got it wrong. That's not who I really am, what I feel I am.

These days, would you believe, I'm confronted with an old man, when I'm not at all sure I've yet left adolescence.

Time mercilessly hones the mirror's efficiency as an instrument of torture. I know it's worse for women, especially those who were once known as fair, though some women magically retain their beauty even in their casket. But the confirmation of deterioration is an androgynous devastation. "One sees oneself in a mirror . . . and each time the desolation of seeing what one sees is stronger than the amazement of having forgotten it," lamented the playwright Luigi Pirandello, whose reflection reminded him of the futility of his infatuation with a much younger woman.

I've become sly about fooling myself before the mirror. "Not too bad," I tell myself, tilting slightly into a more flattering profile. "Don't look quite all my years." Vacation and family-fest photographs bring me up short. There's the undeniable, miserable proof. The shock of recognition: that sallow ancient on the left has to be me. The camera has even less heart than the mirror.

One would think at this stage of life I'd consult a mirror only for necessary business, like shaving, but I pause before almost every glass I pass. Not out of vanity, God no. Just on the off chance that there's been a change for the better, a bit of improvement, in the same way one gets on a scale praying for a loss of a pound or two. Fool that I am. Robert Benchley called his mirror habit an "almost masochistic craving to offend my own aesthetic sense by looking at myself and wincing."

Even when we're young and passably pretty or handsome, the mirror seldom satisfies, because humans placed before any reflecting glass instinctively focus on the imperfections. The skin, the nose, the jutting ears, the hair (or its disappearance), the wrong way it all comes together—something always vexes. A character in Dostoevsky's *The Idiot* laments that if you are unfortunate enough to have a wart on your nose, "you always fancy that no one else has anything else to do in the world than stare at your wart."

I've been told that those who should be most delighted with their mirror images--the celebrated beauties, the models, the movie stars, the *People* people--are the most critical of their looks, because they can't forget that they are in the business of competing with other celebrated beauties. Sophia Loren lamented to a reporter that she felt her nose too big and her chin too short, that sort of bosh.

A full-length mirror is even more mocking. Marilyn Monroe thought her legs too short, her knees too knobby. My own shrine to supreme feminine beauty has always been occupied by Catherine Deneuve, but a character in Richard Stern's novel *Natural Shocks* grumbles about Deneuve's "stick legs." I suppose it's true, but I could adjust. I have little sympathy with Dr. Aylmer in Hawthorne's "The Birthmark," who managed to kill his gorgeous wife in an attempt to remove a minor facial blemish that bugged him, most probably one of those Dostoevskian warts. (Elias Canetti, the Nobel novelist, was bugged, he confessed after his affair with Iris Murdoch, by "the ugliness of her feet.")

Bernie Siegel, the doctor who writes prescriptions for the soul, has suggested that we all stand naked before a full-length mirror for fifteen minutes twice a day, so that we might "learn to love what you see in the mirror." And I thought Siegel didn't have a sense of humor. It would be very hard to love what I see. A daily half hour of looking at that sagging torso would surely send me to a different kind of doctor, perhaps even to a gym. Nah, just forget it. The body is only an envelope, after all, which we all too soon discard. It's the face that reveals the essential soul.

Or does it? Do our features really betray what kind of person we've become, like Dorian Gray's portrait? I hope not, for if the mirror is that perceptive, what I face is an unpleasant truth. I had hoped, even expected, that over such abundant time I would behold, along with the wrinkles, clear evidence of wisdom, serenity and warmth, the kind of grandfatherly film visages we saw when we were growing up—you know, Jean Hersholt, Lionel

Barrymore and Edmund Gwenn. Sorry, but what I see instead is the same gray, protective, unenlightened mask. Try again later.

Often, when I get angry at the mirror for its cruel honesty, I summon a retaliatory response. I make faces, silly contortions, the kind of mugging you think would amuse a five-year-old or that Jim Carrey or Ben Stiller indulge in after teeth-brushing to remind us that they are comedians. I find this silliness quite therapeutic. It erases the image I believe false. It defies the mirror, shows it who's boss. And its irreverence lifts my spirits, by thumbing my nose, as it were, at mere appearance, the superficial, lying surface. After laughing at my cartoon self, I turn away from the sadistic mirror lighter in heart. I have manufactured a gaiety that I try to carry away with me. Not a bad face to show the world.

MEN OF A CERTAIN AGE

●

I don't think I'm imagining this.

I am particularly aware of it on visits to New York, mecca for all of competitive spirit. When I walk past other men of around my age, we eye each other intently, sizing up what we can en passant. Assessments are made, quick grades handed out.

You and I, sir--it is understood in this fleeting glance-- have lived a long time. So how have you made out? How far have you risen? Is your carriage proud, your mien commanding? Do you look prosperous? Satisfied? Even smug? In sum, do you have triumph written all over you, that "beaming content which settles on the faces of men who are successful and are sure of the recognition of their success by everyone," as Tolstoy's Vronsky noted of a fellow officer?

Do I compare myself to, as well as appraise, these strolling gentlemen? Of course I do. I may acknowledge the silliness of this arrogance game, but I'll be damned if I'll be looked down upon either. If I get a sense of projected superiority, I straighten up, rear up really, and try to muster what I hope is a piercing eye. I'll have you know, Mr. Self-satisfied, that I, too, while not rich or notable, have managed to hoist myself up a rung or three.

I confess, too, with appropriate shame, to an ugly pleasure over signs of exhaustion, resignation, defeat, vacancy, even physical infirmity, in a passerby. At least here's one of life's rivals I've bettered.

This is what men do. The jousts go on. I know about the educated, the desk men, but I'm sure it prevails as well with the pool-hall and bowling-alley set. There, money and position can't be the yardstick, but who's been the toughest in a tough world, who's macho most. We can't help ourselves. The male imperative. Why else all those E-mail pitches for penis enhancement? Women don't care. (At least I don't think they do.)

Women, I believe—I understand my rashness in presuming to speak for the other sex--size up other women differently. Appearance is the screen—weight, figure, wrinkles. Hair dyed?

Facelift? It's more how well you have held up than how well you have held up against the world. That's the way I think it's been, anyway. Now that women pursue careers of their own, priorities will doubtless shift. But for my generation, the men were still the primary food gatherers, the urban warriors, the power seekers and wielders. We veterans examine each other for decorations and scars.

This kind of ego wrestling is deplorable, I agree. It shouldn't be this way. Better that when we look at our elders, men or women, we seek evidence of a far different kind of attainment: serenity, self-possession without arrogance, a gentleness in the eyes, an understanding countenance. The rare meeting with such people is startling, because it makes us realize that maybe we A types have got it wrong.

But no, we comfort ourselves, somebody has to strive and struggle, and the toughness becomes ingrained. It's the lifelong driven who accomplish what's needed, who have given us our cities, our cars, our jets, our big and little screens, our comforts, our medical resuscitations. Gentle monks give us jams and liqueurs.

When we men mull over our lifetime achievements, satisfaction is seldom unblemished. One-upmanship may be the overt or hidden agenda when in the company of other males, but garnered laurels seldom rest easy once back in private chambers. Strivers torment themselves with the inevitable peak they failed to reach. Woody Allen would seem to have done well enough for himself, but he recently told a reporter that he "had a much grander conception of where I should wind up in the artistic firmament." No doubt Woody was thinking Ingmar Bergman. But then Bergman probably regretted not being another Dostoyevsky. When it comes to writers, only Shakespeare can rest easy. Or did he envy Sophocles?

Some believe the *ancien régime* of machismo is on the way out, exhausted by all the misery it has brought to the pages of history. A professor in James Lasdun's novel, *The Horned Man*, reflects on "the great repudiation of masculinity that so many of us in academe consider the supreme contribution of the humanities in our time." Masculinity, he elucidates, "in its old, feral, malevolent guise."

So now femininity will replace it, as women rise to empowerment in every sphere and become the new paradigms? I like to think that women, to again risk gender pronouncement, are indeed of a gentler strain, and that they temper ambition with heart. They, too, want to win, but winning will never be all. They have feelings that we don't, and we can only marvel, as John Updike does in *Rabbit at Rest*, at "that strange way women have, of really caring about somebody beyond themselves." Oh, we can make a show of caring. As John Bayley wrote of his late wife, "Iris [Murdoch] is good. I'm not good inside, but I can get by on being nice."

Of course, power's corruptive potential is gender neutral. Martin Amis believes that women have already "made considerable advances in the largely male preserve of self-centeredness." New roles will recreate the old role models, and we'll be back where we started.

Even if a feminized world should turn out a better one, it'll be a good long while before we get there. Whatever Lasdun sees in the academy, off-campus things look different. That is, the same. Men continue to flex and strut and battle and bully, workplace rivals and domestic oppressors. What truly makes one despair are those endless hordes of angry, shouting men, photographed around the globe with upraised rifles, eager to let their elbow-mates know they are men enough to murder in some cause, whether it be holy, unholy or who cares as long as we're males gloriously bonding together.

PASSION, REEL AND REAL

•

I watched the antique film *Bringing Up Baby* the other night. It was of a genre in its time (the thirties) called "screwball comedy." I found it screwball enough ("baby" is a leopard), but mostly un-comic. No matter. I was again in the company of Katherine Hepburn, Cary Grant, Charley Ruggles, Barry Fitzgerald, May Robson, Walter Catlett and a few more names that would mean nothing to you, youngster of 50.

Another memory was jogged, about the way films dealt with the carnal back then, or rather didn't deal with it. Kate and Cary, after the required hour and three-quarters of silly spats, confess their love and embrace. That's it. They don't even kiss. They've never kissed. Fade-out, end of film. That's the way it was in those far-off days.

I was brought up on such purity. Love, marriage itself, were chaste. The sex part was kept secret.

It was certainly kept secret from me. There was no sex education in my school days, God forbid. Or in my home days either. For mom, mum was the word, and papa passed. So I was a late learner, gathering the facts of life not from the gutter—ours was a middle-class neighborhood, I'll have you know—but from a sex manual purchased by my much older brother in preparation for his nuptials and discovered by his prying sibling. Oh no, can this be? I had the usual my-parents-do-this? trauma. I decided I would have no part in such disgusting business. Since I was pre-pubescent at the time, celibacy was a snap.

Today, as anyone who goes to the movies at least once a decade knows, the sex is as common and graphic as the car chase. Off with the clothes, on with the writhing, even before they know each other's last names.

For my generation, the delay, mystery and build-up often led to fumbling, fear and malfunction at the denouement. I sometimes wonder, while sitting unbelieving at the goings-on in my neighborhood Cineplex, what difference it would have made if today's movie frankness had been on exhibit back then.

The films might have provided a beneficial familiarity with the unfamiliar, and served as an instructional aid, like my brother's manual, showing us how to tie the knots, as it were.

But young people today don't need instruction, do they? They are autodidacts. We know that more teenagers are "experimenting" at an ever-younger age. Soon Freud's revelation of infant sexuality will be manifest. After the Big Mac and strawberry shake, other appetites are served. Movies serve as foreplay.

I would imagine, though, that today's X-plicitness presents its own difficulties for these fondling youngsters. The screen bodies, gymnastics and fulfillments are so perfect, actuality has to suffer in comparison. No one in the movies worries about contraception, has nervous hiccups or a sudden urge for the bathroom, is self-conscious about body blemishes or responses, or fails to reach sublimity on cue.

When Hearst Magazines recently brought together the forty women who edit its various national editions of *Cosmopolitan*, those in charge of the French and Swedish mags protested that if they imitate the obsessed U.S. *Cosmo*, circulation in their take-it-or-leave-it lands will plummet. Their readers are bored with the sex topic. So am I. I wish we all were. Maybe then we could rid ourselves of sex saturation in our films, sit-coms, maga-zines, novels, ads and talk shows.

I like to think, too, that were the subject to become a yawn, the movies could return to their old gentility. We could have romance again, not the mechanics. Let the embrace and the kiss once more define the happy ending. The follow-through doesn't have to be acted out, turning us all into discomfited voy-eurs. We know all this, you don't have to show us again, like the stewardess explaining how our seat belts work.

Quaint of me, eh? Hopeless, squeamish fogy, you say. A relic. Can't himself be honest, face the facts of life. If sex is a part of everyday life, why not portray it on screen, as we do people eating a sandwich or cleaning out the garage?

Simple modesty, that's why. Since the expulsion from Eden, reticence has been inbred. For some personal, bodily busi-ness, you shut the door. And you should.

But enough. If you don't agree with me, I'll not convince you. It's a generational thing. Anyway, you'll have to excuse me. I'm in the middle of a Doris Day-Rock Hudson video.

IS A DOLLAR EARNED

•

At one point in Eugene O'Neill's *Long Day's Journey Into Night*, the father, James Tyrone, admonishes his family for not turning off lights when they leave a room. "I never claimed one bulb costs much. It's having them on, one here and one there, that makes the Electric Light Company rich." Every time I've seen the play, the audience laughs.

Why? What's funny? I see nothing to laugh at. My own mother used practically the same words as father Tyrone, and I've been faithful to her memory and enduring wisdom. And aside from enriching the electric company, light bulbs cost a lot more than when she was alive.

Many's the night I've awakened at 2 am, troubled by something, to realize what's bothering me is the light I left burning in the hall. If I get through the night and discover my oversight only the next morning, my mood is sour. Philosophy advises me not to cry over spilt electricity, but I am not yet an accomplished philosopher.

My wife lacks my sensibility and Spartan discipline. I am constantly flicking switches where she has just been. This lamentable failing in an otherwise admirable woman is probably the greatest strain on our marriage and may, after more than thirty years of bliss, trigger a separation, so that I can at last take total control of the amperage consumption in my domestic environment.

That may strike you as a rather trivial reason for discord, but one mustn't minimize the seemingly minor irritations that can threaten even the closest relationships. I remember a woman confessing to a television interviewer that it drove her to distraction over the years that when she brought home a bunch of grapes, her husband would pick them off one by one as he passed the bowl, leaving ugly, stubbly stalks, whereas she always neatly scissored off a whole stem. I believe a marriage counselor had to be called in, who resolved the issue, but at considerable expense.

Returning to the topic of wattage consumption, yes, we

old folk are skinflints, tightwads, stingy, miserly, grasping, cheap, chintzy, whatever you want to call us (I prefer "frugal). And that's true no matter how much money we've stashed away in municipals.

It's not that we're mean-spirited. Just realistic and self-protective. Terrified, really. The specter of what-ifs. What if Medicare goes bankrupt? What if inflation goes berserk and the value of my savings is sliced in half? What if I live to 102? What if I need round-the-clock care from the age of 84 to 102? What if they (never mind who "they" are) want to put me away in a nursing home from hell?

So we pinch—yes—our every penny. Each cent saved is a contribution to our personal peace-of-mind fund.

Look, who doesn't like to save a bit, whatever our age? I think of those luminous instances when I parked my car and found that the previous occupant of the space had left me twenty-five minutes on the meter. A petty windfall no doubt, but I felt for a moment that the gods knew me and were revealing their pleasure.

The writer John Mortimer tells of a rich uncle who flew into a rage when Mortimer's aunt made a grocery list on a new envelope. I should hope so. I fish used envelopes out of the waste basket if I need, say, to jot down a phone number and I am not in my study. When at my desk, I am equipped. As a writer, I generate countless discarded pages, and I scissor any blank lower halves into 3x5's. I also snitch note pads from hotel rooms. The little shampoo ampules, too, if you want to report me. No need to purloin ashtrays anymore. No one who comes to our house smokes. That nasty habit is now reserved for the lower classes, not our sort of guest list.

There are so many little ways we can save a nickel here and a quarter there, building our own private social security system. It goes without saying that one should buy the generics, clip the Sunday supplement coupons, go to movies in the afternoon and use a bar of soap until it disappears. In my house we wash and reuse Zip-lock storage and freezer bags until either (a) the zip-lock loses its zip or (b) the plastic crumbles into shreds. I deny, however—I've heard the calumnies—that we wash and reuse paper towels.

Purse-string control has nothing to do with one's wealth. I don't like to gossip, but I've been told by a quite reliable source that John D. Rockefeller would switch to an old golf ball when a new one landed near a water hole. I personally happen to know a very rich family that carefully smoothes out, stores and reuses Christmas wrappings. Of course, one can go too far. You may not have heard about Hettie Green, the richest woman in America when she died in 1916. Her son lost a leg because she kept insisting that he didn't really need a pricey operation.

I know that's madness, but I have to admit that I am guilty of a similar craziness. I have an unreliable back, yet I'll carry a heavy suitcase rather than tip a porter. When walking in another city and my back begins to act up, I keep going, grumbling, rather than pay for a taxi. My petty parsimony is going to cost me dearly one of these days, but I can't seem to help myself. To scatter coin when there's a cost-free alternative goes against my grain.

In the realm of coin-scattering, all tipping irks me. Why this surcharge, this supplemental sales tax? I don't deny that those who provide a service deserve compensation—which I would prefer their employers supply in decent sufficiency—but if I can avoid being a recipient of that service, so much the better. Suitcases with wheels are a marvelous scientific breakthrough. They enable me to hurry, somewhat shamefacedly, past any hotel attendant who offers assistance. If when leaving the hotel I absolutely need a taxi, I stroll a block away and hail one myself. Why give a dollar to a doorman for waving his arm and opening a door?

Cafeterias seem to have disappeared, but fast-food and take-out eateries don't expect tips. At least they didn't until Starbucks came along, with its begging bowls by the register. Anyway, who but a feckless profligate would pay three bucks for a cup of coffee?

The truth is, though, that when we old folks really want something, we cough up readily enough. "I worked hard all my life, and you now want me to drive a Kia, stay at a Motel 6, drink Two-Buck Chuck wine, sit in the balcony, take an inside cabin without a porthole? How can you be so heartless?"

Happily in my case, I can afford such little luxuries, thanks to the money I've saved on electricity all these years.

THRIFT OR SPENDTHRIFT?

●

There's another motive for thrift in the winter years when we're spending without earning what we're spending. We hate to think we could leave our children a bare cupboard.

Of course, those who have amassed mountains of money, and will never run out of it even if they live as long as Mickey Mouse, needn't fuss about outflows. They worry, instead, about leaving the kids—who will themselves probably be grey-haired when the will is read—too much of the stuff. They want their children to have enough to be able to live in gated communities and be listed as donors in the symphony program but not so much that they will forego labor and do naught but twiddle their golf clubs and swizzle their Pimm's Cups.

That's not my problem, probably not yours. At least

Forbes has not bothered to tap into my bank account to find out if I belong on its annual list of the ludicrously rich. Once retired, our accountants told us that if we lived another actuarial 23 ½ years and earned 4.8 percent on our nest egg, we could take one ten-day cruise a year, go to Atlantic City for three nights and lose $275 at the tables, dine at an outrageously overpriced restaurant on our birthdays, wedding anniversary and special celebratory events, like the death of Patrick Buchanan. We should make out okay if we die when we're supposed to, but we'd risk leaving our offspring nothing but photo albums, a heaping treasury of memories.

It's a tempting course. One fantasizes about calling in one's sons and daughters and their spouses and declaring something like this: "Your mother and I want you to know where you stand. Well, here it is, in plainest English. We provided you with food and a bed and many pairs of shoes, paid for your education, took you and your children to Disney World not once but twice, and bought you a side-by-side refrigerator when the old one died and a sump pump when your basement flooded. We therefore consider our responsibility to you has been met. The good news is that we believe we have enough to get by so that we'll never be a burden to you. And there is the life insurance policy we took out when you were small and $25,000 seemed like a lot of money, a sum to split among the lot of you. But beyond that there'll be little you can expect. We both worked hard all our lives. Go thou and do likewise. Put money in thy purses. For whatever time and stamina are left us, we'll be shouting encouragement from the sidelines."

That's what we'd like to say to them, boldly, without flinching, and then board the plane for the Italian Riviera. But we can't. We love them, damn it, and you want to do as much as you can for those you love. But how much is "much" and how much is "too much"?

With every expenditure that could be called not-really-necessary or even smacking of luxury, one's conscience—or at least consciousness—pipes up. Should I economize so they won't have to? Should I fly business class or go economy class so they can remain comfortably middle class? Or possibly attain higher rank in the suburban hierarchy? As my friend Mike Stolper, a wise financial counselor to the wealthy, has said, "Sometimes we have to choose between living well now or enabling our grandchildren to live like royalty."

And don't fool yourself: expectations tickle the minds of our heirs, probably on a daily schedule. "We love you, mommy and daddy, and want you to live forever and ever, but lord, what a sweet relief it would be if we could get out from under this mountain of debt. And it's not really for ourselves that we've extended ourselves. We'd be happiest living in a one bedroom apartment in a part of town where there's not even a Starbucks. It's for our kids—your grandchildren—that we've splurged. We bought this ridiculously big house so that they would have a happy childhood in a good neighborhood, with a big yard for their Olympic-sized swimming pool and municipal-park-sized playground equipment. We've hired Cirque du Soleil performers for their birthday parties so they can invite their classmates without shame. And we will send them to universities that will make them feel superior for the rest of their lives. We hope to continue to support them as they establish their careers as documentary film producers and artists who work only in bricks, sheet rock and milk cartons."

Don't look to me for spending guidelines. I agonize, a little, then pull out the credit card. Maybe I'll die before my actuarial time and leave at least a little something in the pot. If not, there are a few tangible assets for my three sons to divvy up. Rows and rows of books, not all of them paperbacks, containing wisdom beyond the worth of pearls. A pair of gold cuff links, one for each of two of my sons; the third will have to be content with my Mont Blanc pencil. There's one good watch, worth at least $500; they can draw straws for that. My car, I mustn't forget my car, though by the time I expire, it will no doubt have done the same.

So I deny myself little, but not without heartburn when I choose the Lexus over the Toyota, Paul Stuart over Land's End, Martha's Vineyard over Red Bank, and Prague over Williamsburg . My conscience will catch up with me, I know it. I'll spend my last days in my counting house, ruing my selfishness, desperately toting up what remains, wondering if my ancient body parts would fetch some trifle in the medical market.

But if all's spent, I'll just have to face the fact that all I will leave my beloved children is disappointment. I hope I can meet that possibility with stoic resolve. I recommend they prepare themselves to do the same.

THE TIME SLIDE

•

You're only as old as you feel, we're told with exasperating regularity. But it's true. When you feel like hell a good deal of the time, you know precisely how things stand.

Put six people past 70 in a room and listen to them. For at least the first hour they'll talk about nothing but their un-health.

These are the same friends, mind you, who only a few years ago dismissed health inquiries with a "fine-fine" shrug and hurried on to chatter about their children. What else was there to talk about then, unless it were a presidential election year? One had work and children and work that involved the children, leaving little time for anything else. Since you weren't likely to chat about your office's cash flow crisis at the dinner table, you compared notes on schools and pediatricians and summer camps and soccer coaches and tae kwon do classes and maddening progeny behavior and misbehavior, followed all too soon by reviews of college possibilities. As novelist David Lodge has noted, "Literature is mostly about having sex and not much about having children. Life is the other way around."

Our seventy-and-plus-year-olds still say a few words about their "kids," who are now in their forties or even fifties and living at least 2,000 miles distant. One brags a bit about a daughter's thriving medical practice and a grandson's golfing prowess, but nobody goes on for long, sensing the data of little interest to anyone else. One sometimes wonders how much it even interests oneself. The offspring have sprung far, and their off-site lives are hazier than memories of their younger days.

No, conversation among the elderly now hovers around the fever charts of the assembled and their mutual friends. "How's it going, Hank?" "Not too bad," Hank replies, then proceeds to tick off a dozen current afflictions starting at the eyes and neck and working his way down. Then each of the others follows with a recitation of ailments and breakdowns and repairs underway— the specialists, the treatments, the surgeries, the therapies, the replacements, the medications, the whole dreary, boring lot. The others listen politely, nodding their heads in sympathy, waiting their turn at dolorous enumeration. Anyone who's been in the hospital within the last month is the undeclared winner.

One bodily malfunction that isn't mentioned--except for an occasional smirky wisecrack--is the waning of sexual desire and prowess. The itch may still be there, but the scratching has become problematic.

At least this was true until Viagra came along. Now we can perform unto death.

Ads for the wonder drug show older couples with sly smiles, implying the wife is thankful her husband can again make her whole. It has occurred to me, however, that many a wife may curse the day Viagra was conceived. One had one's youth of passion, then the consequenccs of that passion to raise to adulthood, and now one would as soon be left in peace, to read a novel or finish a sudoku. But lord, there he is again, with his self-congratulatory tumescent arrogance, ready to beat his chest and play the ape. As one Englishwoman sighed, sex again, "raises its ugly head."

Men, on the other hand, are presumably overjoyed by the arrival of this pharmaceutical marvel. I wonder if we should be. Isn't enough enough? Recall Plato's reporting that when the playwright Sophocles was asked if he were still enjoying sex, he famously replied, "Hush, man, I am delighted to have escaped from that, like a slave who has run away from a wild and crazy master." Sensible man. At our age we really should be thinking about something else besides what we've been thinking about most of our waking hours (and a good many sleeping ones) since the age of fourteen.

Time to quiet the tomtoms and listen to the choir. After all, our Maker awaits.

WHAT'S UP DOC?

●

As soon as I'd retired, people felt compelled to ask me how I now occupied my time. "Visiting doctors," I'd answer honestly.

The calendar squares blacken with such appointments as the years gather. The machinery breaks down and one goes in ever more often for repairs. I wish my rollover IRA had grown as fast as my portfolio of specialists.

I suspect a good many consultations are sought just for the opportunity of a listening ear. It's satisfying, even healing, to have someone to complain to. Many people marry primarily for that very reason. But after years of endless repetitions about assorted ills, spouses either tune out or look at you with a kind of pity you weren't asking for. Doc is paid to listen.

Many times I have left a doctor's office feeling better even though I haven't even filled the prescription yet. It's as though unburdening one's ailments leaves some part of them behind. The doctor may be indifferent to your suffering—after all, he's got a waiting room full of pain—but even pretended sympathy ameliorates. There is still something of the shaman about doctors. They don't dance around in feathered headdresses chanting mantras, but they've got the white robe, the stethoscope, the machinery with lots of dials, the Gothic-type diplomas on the wall, a cache of magic-pill samples and a lofty air of authority. Clearly they have been given the power to cure. Demons are thereby exorcised.

I have friends who don't agree. Their doctors can't make them feel sweet sixteen again, so what good are they? "Doctors! Ha! What do they know?" I think they know a great deal, at least enough that I am willing to put my very life in their hands. I am quite fond of my doctors—good, caring souls, all of them.

In my earlier years, I was not so perceptive. The truth is, I was most uncharitable. Doctor-baiting was one of my favorite pastimes.

Do you know, I'd huff, that I had to wait an hour and a

quarter in my internist's reception room the other day, with nothing to do but sneer at year-old *Sports Illustrated*s, the bathing suit issue missing? The President of the United States wouldn't have treated me with such discourtesy. But doctors think they're above presidential. They're imperial.

And the money they make! In my mind they made more than anybody. What did I know back then of the sacks of gold heaped on partners in legal and accounting firms and stuffed into the limo trunks of Wall Street and corporate executives? It was only when a "total compensation" of hundreds of thousands turned into one of hundreds of millions that the secret hit the front pages.

Well, if it's their comeuppance I wanted, I got it. Doctors have been dethroned, reduced, humbled. Now I pity all persevering practitioners.

The average medical man today can still afford to eat out once a week, I'm sure, but his income is probably no better than a bagel-store owner's. In the days when I was so indignant, doctors could charge pretty much what they wanted. Suppose you needed an operation for a suspicious-looking tumor. What were you supposed to do, haggle about the fee, then stalk out and go over to the funeral parlor to see how much you'd save if you skipped the surgery? No, no, you'd plead, for God's sake, take the damn thing out, whatever it costs! But insurance companies and government agencies—also known as third parties--are not in the least excited by a tumor. "We'll pay you a fair price, doc, but don't get greedy on us." I tell you, the power has shifted.

Then there's the quagmire of Medicare, Medicaid, HMOs, PPOs and bureaucratic horrors that I, a layman, know nothing about. In every medical office I enter I see a half-dozen Bartlebys per doctor, all stumbling along vast paper trails. No wonder so many doctors have thrown in their rubber gloves and retired to Tucson.

Those who do labor on must do so out of an irresistible urge to heal, bless them. And they do enjoy other compensations. After all, a doctor is a doctor and not a mere mister. We have no heredity titles in this country, and few of any other kind. I don't consider Coach Smith or Senator Jones titles. An earl is always an earl, but the coach and senator quickly lose their status if they don't perform to the public's satisfaction. "Professor" is a title people pretend to respect, while secretly contemptuous of someone viewed as unfit for life and therefore sentenced to spend it reading books. "Reverend," too, is a title, but priests, ministers and rabbis are at the mercy of their audiences. We understand and can critique a sermon, but we aren't likely to challenge a diagnosis of osteomyelitis or tularemia.

"Doctor" remains a respected title. "Physician" sounds even better, don't you agree? Maybe because it echoes "physicist," of whom all non-physicists are in awe. (Dr. Freud, according to Ernest Jones, sincerely doubted his intellectual capacity because he couldn't understand what the hell Einstein was going on about.) You may think of a "doctor" as the proprietor of a body shop, but a "physician" is one with a wisdom that transcends the healing arts. It probably goes back to the Middle Ages, when court physicians like Averroës and Maimonides were also big-shot philosophers.

It would be nice, come to think of it—as the years pile on urgencies--to have one's personal physician, like the kings and caliphs of yore and the dictators of our own time. "Doc, I woke up this morning with an ache here, near the shoulder. And a sort of a stabbing pain when I raise my arm. My neck's a little stiff, too, when I turn it this far. Wha'd'ya think—heat, cold, rest, some stretches? And could you take a look at my throat? It was sort of scratchy when I woke up this morning. Hope I'm not coming down with something just before the Caribbean cruise. Oh, yeah, another thing . . ."

But I'll not complain. I've put together a splendid team of my own court physicians. I'll never leave them—no retiring to Tucson for me--and to make sure they don't leave me for a place more divine than Arizona, I pick them younger than myself. They'll be around to preserve me until the fateful hour.

As for that particular appointment, I do not mind if I'm kept waiting.

YOUR TROUBLES ARE BEHIND YOU

●

Postulate: Everyone who has a back sooner or later has a bad back. The later, the badder.

The term "back" is imprecise. In my case, its territory starts with arthritic pain through the shoulders and extends to sciatic pain that goes right down my leg in search of my big toe. In between isn't so good either, thanks to something called spinal stinosis, which sounds fatal but is instead lifelong.

"Pain," too, has fluctuating dimensions. It varies from aches that a night's sleep puts to rest to horrific spasms that a week's rest doesn't put to sleep.

I'm willing to make a sizeable bet that I've seen more back doctors than you have. Not that the number matters, because the routine is always the same. Each sends me out for X-rays, an

MRI (invented, I believe, by Darth Vader) and sometimes a CAT scan. I bring the outsize floppy negatives back to the doctor, who clamps them on a screen, points to ghostly shapes and tells me, with solemn authority, why my back hurts. So? I know it hurts, what do I do about it? You're a doctor, cure me.

He looks at me with pity but no compassion. Sorry, but your bones are stacked against you. Stretches, exercises, multiple trips to Lourdes aren't going to change the reality of that picture up there. Live on Aleve, and when it gets so bad you can no longer make it from your bed to the bathroom, come see me again. He smiles farewell. The knife awaits.

But we've all known people who have had back surgery, once, twice, even thrice, and who still walk as though a nail is sticking up in one shoe. Desperation dictates we try something else first.

More accurately, somethings, plural. Let's compare notes. How many of these have you shared with me? Chiropractors? Physical therapists? Trainers? Massage? Yoga? Pilates? Tai Chi? Acupuncture? Prayer? Would you like to consult my library of books on spinal rehabilitation? View my get-a better-back-in four-weeks videos? Come, let's lie down on the floor together.

Bring your knees up to your chinny, chin, chin, that's a good girl. Now arch your back, raise your head and shoulders, bring your right leg over your left leg and your left leg over your right and . . . What? You're having difficulty? If you could do this stuff, you wouldn't need to? All right, then, stop.

I stopped about two years ago. No more stretches, weights, bungee straps and prone pretzeling, and I feel not a whit worse. Nor a whit better either, but I have more time for Free Cell.

The one stretch I still do I learned not from a doctor or therapist but from a bellhop (do they still call them bellhops?) at a New York hotel. I watched this old fellow juggling suitcases that must have weighed fifty pounds each, and I cornered him in the elevator. He was 64, he told me, about to retire, and had never had serious back trouble "Tell me, oh rare and wondrous one, what's your secret?" "Dunno. Just been that way. Sometimes I get a little achy, and I just put my fists on my hips and bend back a little," the oldest remedy in the book. So now after washing dishes or folding laundry--bending over anything lower than a bistro bar is a killer, isn't it?--I do as the man said, simultaneously adding some shoulder shrugs. Ah, that's better. Now I can finish scrubbing that damn frying pan.

One gym I frequented when still in a pro-active mode, had just acquired a device that would remind anyone of an electric chair, and I agreed—I must have been particularly despairing that week--to play guinea pig. They strapped me into the thing and told me to bend forward slowly as far as I could, my stretched back evidently lifting gunnysacks of lead. After the fourth session I decided that it may not have been an electric chair, but the end result, should I continue, would be the same. About a year later the place called me. They'd thrown out my chair and acquired a new and better model. Would I like to come over and try it out? My answer was not polite.

Many years ago a *New York Magazine* reporter touted a book, *Mind Over Back Pain*, by Dr. John Sarno. The reporter claimed that thanks to Dr. Sarno's insights, he had gone from incapacitated to running marathons with his seven-year-old son on his shoulders, or something like that. I made an appointment to see Dr. Sarno. He assured me that I would be fine if I followed his advice, which would take too long to dispense in a mere $50 consultation (this was some time ago, remember) and if I would be so kind as to write a check for ten times that amount I was welcome to attend two evening lectures at which he would make everything clear. About two hundred of us sufferers listened to the guru explain that our back pain was really only in our minds. People with similar back formations who didn't realize they were supposed to be in pain were leading wholly normal lives. Go into denial and all will be well.

I know the mind wields considerable clout over the body. Why else does seeing a waterfall make me want to go to the bathroom? They were sawing down a tree in my neighbor's yard the other day and the buzzing reminded me of a dentist's drill and three teeth began to ache. But I failed Dr. Sarno and his think-positive charisma. My back pain triumphed over my wimpish mind.

Like me, you're no doubt a back shopper, unable to resist a store or catalog that promises relief. I've bought contoured pillows, back cushions, seat cushions, ergonomic chairs, braces, braces with magnets, insoles with magnets, massagers, amulets and philters. But the critical quest has always been for the perfect mattress. Eight hours cradled in its therapeutic embrace would surely set me up for pain-free days.

Once it was laid down that we lie down on hardness. If you were too fussy to sleep on the floor, you were advised to get the firmest mattress you could find. For years, at a doctor's behest, I slept with a board under my firm mattress, thus replicating a floor. That was about the same time that dentists were telling us hard toothbrushes were the most effective, until they realized their patients' tooth enamel was disappearing. Hard toothbrushes and hard mattresses were thrown out of the textbooks and my house at about the same time.

But though ultra-firm was out, mushy wouldn't do either. Something in-between, a mattress obliging but not obsequious. The search began.

Trying on mattresses is a frustrating business. "Go ahead, it's all right, lie down on it, see how it feels," the store clerk urges. But you are not expected to fall asleep for eight hours, as you would do if you wrapped it up and took it home. It's hard to judge the character of anything in fifty seconds flat.

I've changed mattresses more often over the last twenty years than I have cars. I passed on a water mattress, though. I consider them suitable only for Hugh Hefner. I was looking for rest, not a playground.

But I did sleep on an air mattress for a couple of years. I figured I could experiment with the air pressure until I found the perfect degree of firmness, and ever after enjoy pneumatic bliss. Trouble was, the mattress was fickle. I guess it was the heat of my body and blankets, but the mattress would inhale during the night and swell up, until for the last couple of hours of sleep, I might as well have had my old board back. A thrift shop spurned the thing, so I punctured it.

One mattress boutique I found in Manhattan wanted something like $4,000 for its top number. Why impoverish myself, I asked the clerk. What's so special? "Uniquely, our mattresses are hand-assembled," she informed me. Okay, that's nice, but so what? I'm looking for relief, not an artifact.

I also tried out one of those "memory foam" mattresses, widely advertised as "developed by NASA." I didn't know so many astronauts had bad backs. This mattress, which promises proper posture for the supine spine, was also expensive, so I opted instead for a mattress topper three inches thick made of the same stuff, figuring my hips, though well developed, shouldn't sink more than three inches. But I found that a straight back at night is not necessarily a happy back in the morning. Topper disappeared.

I finally settled on a semi-firm mattress that cleverly

comes with a marshmallow-y topping, what they call a pillow-top mattress. I don't know that it's any better a nurse to my back than its predecessors, but it is very comfy. I cherish it so much that I validate Dr. Sarno: My mind is pleased so my back feels better. On those mornings when I wake up unable to deny that my mattress has failed me, I am very vexed with it. But I quickly forgive it. After all, maybe I was to blame, tossing this way and that during a ridiculous nightmare about invading terrorists.

When friends ask me how my back and I are getting along, I always answer that some days are not so bad and other days not so good. Wishy-washy, I know, but accurate. And if the pendulum swings in no wider arc, I can live with my condition. In fact, my goal is to live with it with until I am no longer living. It is a contest: Who will come first, the grim surgeon or the Grim Reaper?

HONEY, HAVE YOU SEEN MY ENERGY ANYWHERE?

•

I don't have any statistics around the place, but I'm pretty sure most husbands are a couple of years older than their wives. Often, as in my own case, quite a few years older.

In the early years of marriage, the age gap is scarcely noticed. Both parties are too busy scrambling over life's hurdles. But as the years roll out, the wife gets old, and hubby gets *really* old.

The trouble begins.

She's ready for a movie. He's ready for bed. In the same vein, she'd like an afternoon of golf, and he'd like a nap. She's interested in learning Italian and invites him to come along. He says English has always been good enough for him and it'll stay that way. She's on a fund-raising committee at church. He refuses to go to any meetings, anywhere, for any reason, period. She keeps up with what's going on in the world, and he complains he can't get the Sunnis and Shiites straight, and who cares anyway. The world's been a mess for his entire lifetime and will no doubt stay that way, and what's for lunch?

He feels like dog on a leash being yanked away from a comfy spot before the fire. She feels like the mistress of a dog who's too stiff and lazy to sniff the outside air.

More and more often, she'll give up and go out for a show or a meal with a girlfriend, leaving him at home to grumble. She's even gone with the same friend to a five-day cooking school in San Francisco. He's happy to have the house to himself. He finally gets around to caulking the shower and manages to round up an afternoon poker game, but spends most of his time reading the paper and watching TV. For dinner, it's take-out barbecue (skip the salad), two beers, the semi-finals and an early bed.

Vacations are a good indicator of the state of the union. She's hot to trot and he wonders if he wants to go any further than Blockbuster's. So she does all the planning and makes all the arrangements. She's getting brochures about a walking tour of Ireland. He looks over her shoulder and complains that it wears him out to walk from the airline check-in counter to the departure gate.

She finally gets him on a cruise to the Greek Islands. She does the land tours while he stays behind and plays the slots.

If they travel by car, she usually takes the wheel—and loads and unloads the trunk, fills the tank when needed, and pops unto a deli for the coffee. You'll often see her giving him a hand getting out of the car.

There's something else even harder for her to take. She tries to stay optimistic and cheerful and find things to look forward to. He's become dour and testy, with long bouts of silence.

When a couple divorce after twenty-five years of marriage, the breakup can often be laid at the proverbial male midlife crisis. He convinces himself he is infatuated with, and rejuvenated by, a younger woman, as novels repeatedly confirm. When the split comes after forty years of marriage, I wonder if it isn't often the other way around. She wants a spryer mate, or, more likely, no anchor mate at all.

I am quite aware of the shoals I now navigate in my own household, and I have no intention of allowing a bust-up. I feign interest in all matters my younger wife deems worthy of interest. I accompany her to all--well, almost all—performances of drama, music and dance, ready to be elbowed if I snore. I limp after her in museums and ancient ruins. I am ready for Scrabble, though I draw the line at Trivial Pursuit, since I can't remember the names of anything. I try not to yawn too often or ostentatiously before 10 pm.

I offer to help with chores, like garage clean-up, praying that she will refuse. I manage to keep most of my aches and pains to myself, knowing how tiresome are complainers. I attend dinners and parties, and rehearse beforehand the names of people I've known for twenty-five years who are likely to show up. And I bone up on the news so I'll have something to say when the white wine is passed around. I try my best to stand up straight, or as perpendicular as I can.

This subterfuge and denial, I know, cannot go on forever. Already I flounder, I stagger, I occasionally collapse. From time to time she looks at her flagging, sagging husband and I know she must be thinking that before long she'll be playing nursemaid.

I do feel sorry for younger wives, not excluding my own. Of course they didn't consider, way back when they said "I do," what the "doing" could eventually entail. Their dewy, naive love will now be tested.

Most will pass the test, I'm sure. Women are far more forbearing, caring and sacrificing than men. Still, there are limits, even to love. So we'd better put our best bunioned foot forward and act out the sprightliest show we can. Some roses now and then wouldn't be a bad strategy either.

DON'T KNOW WHAT MAKES THE
WHEELS GO ROUND

•

The more years that go too-swiftly by, the more I am out-gadgeted. Adult playthings multiply and pile up in stores and catalogs. But not around me. I do not have, nor do I wish to have, a laptop, an iPod, a Palm, a Black Berry, a TiVo, a digital camera, a camcorder, a hand-held TV, a GPS, a Bluetooth, a satellite radio, a portable DVD player, or some combination toy that does all of the above, plus picks winning horses, and weighs only ten ounces. I do have a cell phone so I can call for help in case I drive into a tree, and I have learned to operate the microwave oven. Beyond that, I am oblivious of the overflowing cornucopia of electronic wonders.

Three remotes sit on the table before my TV, VCR and DVD, and I can never remember which controls what, what four-fifths of the buttons are for, or how to accomplish even the basics, like watching the movie at the point where I left off instead of having to start from the beginning again. I suspect I could perform all necessary operations with just one of the three instruments, but I am not eager to return to school for a degree in programming.

I am writing this confessional on my computer, but I'm incapable of summoning up the half--nay, the quarter--of the awesome powers that I know are buried within its bowels. There are buttons and dials in my car that remain a mystery to me, after driving the thing for five years. A card on the desk in my hotel room the other day informed me that I could "launch your web browser," and I haven't the slightest idea what generous offer I had spurned.

I know a few people my age who have kept up, sort of. They are at least far more knowledgeable than I about computers. I have other age peers who don't even own an answering machine. It's annoying when I call them and can't leave a message, but I admire their valiant resistance to the incursions of the inhuman. And--if you can believe this--they actually write letters! I mean on stationery!

Aside from the fact that I wouldn't be able to operate the

thingamajigs if I owned them, they leave me cold. Maybe it has something to do with the fact that when you and I were growing up we didn't have video and computer games for after-school delinquency. It might have acclimatized me to electronic wizardry. But life was primitive back then. I still evoke a chuckle from my wife when I sometimes absent-mindedly refer to our refrigerator as an ice-box. Fans were our only form of air conditioning. I remember as a lad helping my mother wash clothes with a scrub-board and wringer—I felt adult-important cranking the rollers-- and hang them on a line with clothes pegs. The word "digital," if used at all, had something to do with fingers. Now it seems to have usurped the universe.

The truth is, I have never been much for science generally, and, therefore, its artifacts. I shift the blame for my illiteracy in this branch of knowledge to a missing gene. Chapters and verse have always been my thing. Stephen Hawking is not my bedtime reading. When I was forced in my school years to study science, I was hopeless. I flunked high school physics—well, the teacher donated a passing D after exasperating weeks of after-school tutoring. A science course was required in college, too, and I thumbed desperately through the catalog until I found one with no lab requirement—anthropology, where I was told that bones and fossils prove that man descended—ascended?—from apes. This I had no trouble believing.

A couple of years ago I took my nine-year-old grand-daughter to the Air and Space Museum in Washington. While she was absorbed in finding out what she would weigh on Mars—a statistic that has never particularly troubled me—I wandered off to the side and studied the panels explaining how airplanes fly. I vaguely remember hearing the same myth in those tortuous phys-ics classes. Air flowing under the wings creates a high-pressure area that, in obedience to the indomitable laws of nature, pushes up toward the lower-pressure area above the wings, lifting the whole apparatus sky-high. Or something like that. I'm sure you know the mechanics better than I.

I could only shake my head. They expect me to believe that a draft under the wings lifts that huge machine, weighing Google-knows how many tons, carrying passengers and luggage weighing more tons? Aw, come on now. If you ask me, I'd say there is no way man can fly. Just give up the idea. Settle for hot-air balloons. Or try inventing something else, like a ship that moves under water.

My granddaughter and I also visited a planetarium, where we learned how our universe began. You know the story. Seems that about fourteen billion years ago—I think I've got the zeros right—there occurred what astrophysicists playfully call the Big Bang. Fourteen billion years, mind, give or take a week or two. I suppose I am not the best qualified person to quarrel with an astrophysicist, but how can they know what happened fourteen billion years ago? Fess up guys, admit you've hazarded a wild guess after a night of too much bourbon and too little sleep. For my money, what they're feeding us is harder to swallow than what the Creationists believe. At least I can understand the Biblical version.

That's the way it's always been with me, you see. I just don't get it, any of it. Computers, television, fax machines, the Internet, CD players, CAT scanners, cars, electric lights, telephones, ball point pens, water that flows from a tap—you name it, they're all mysteries to me, miracles that outclass the burning bush and the loaves and fishes.

I know I should repair the holes in my education, but the truth is, I'd have it no other way. I live in a world of the inexplicable. I am surrounded by wonders. If I understood it all, where would be the magic, the splendor, the awe? My ignorance is my bliss. Mountains are monumental and canyons grand, but what man has made is what gives me intimations of the supernatural. Could God be revealed in the microchip?

TO ELBA WITH GOOGLE

•

He (me, in third-person guise): "We need a birthday present for Charley, and I think he'd like the new Franklin biography. I'll stop by Barnes and Noble on my way home."

She (the wife): Let me order it from Amazon. It'll be here in plenty of time, and there are a couple of paperbacks I want."

He: "The library's still open. I'm driving over. Got a few things to look up.

She: "Why don't you try the web first?"

He: Blast it, I threw out Sunday's double crostic by mistake.

She: So? Get it off the web.

The web, the web, the web! We're all caught in the web, trapped in the Internet, moored to the monitor. Never leave home without it, vow the laptop luggers. In fact, there's no need to ever leave home at all. Don't go out, go on-line. We've got the world on a cable.

I suppose it's one more evidence of the calcification of aging that I resist this wonder of the age. My wife has adapted because she is a good deal younger than I. But maybe it's also because I have some remnant of humanity left in me. Faces have more appeal than icons, and I'd rather speak than click.

I also like books, damn it. I have a couple thousand around here to prove it. I don't want to look something up on the computer. I want to pull out a volume of my treasured *Encyclopedia Britannica* and hold the thing in my hands, weighty with authority. Looking up something in an encyclopedia, an almanac, a biographical dictionary, an anthology, an atlas or any other reference work is a satisfaction instilled from childhood, yours and mine. We knew print, not pixels. Like an archeologist, I go to a site and dig. A screen search may bring the same results, but the experience itself is thin, devoid of the resonance, propriety and purity of long custom.

A web search is faster, more efficient? I don't know about that. Suppose there is some aspect of the French Revolution I want to research. In a book I could find it quickly, led by chronology and instinct. When I fed the Internet with "French Revolution," it came up with 1,624,910 "results." See how long that takes to whittle down, web worshipper.

Besides, when I check out something in a book, my eye inevitably strays to other paragraphs, other pages. One makes discoveries, chances upon the intriguing, the informative, perhaps the inspiring. Printed pages are seductive. The screen leaves me cold.

As a writer who never reached the semi-finals in spelling bees, I do find my computer's spell-check feature useful. But if it's a nuanced definition I want, I respectfully rise to stand before my unabridged, noble on its wooden stanchion, and turn the pages with the solemnity of a monk at his breviary. Here lies authority, the last word, so to speak. And should I need further elucidation, I bring out my massive *Compact Oxford English Dictionary* and the magnifying glass that reveals its centuries of scholarship in miniscule type. Hunched over the volume, glass in hand, I feel like a dedicated scientist researching the nuclei of etymology.

No doubt these tomes, along with Roget, Bartlett and the other standard aide-de-campus references, can be imbedded in one's hard drive, but I want these holy objects in palpable form at my elbow. They are my trustworthy companions, standing close by, ever ready to serve. They aren't turned off at night. Their physical presence reassures me that my world, at least, is in order.

I like libraries. I've lived a considerable portion of my life in them. They are civilized refuges. People behave because they are there with similar serious intent. All the world's knowledge surrounds us. I am at peace in a library. I belong, like an alcoholic in a bar or a general in battle. What aura does a CD Rom exude?

Nor do I want to buy a book from a warehouse in cyberspace. I'll find any excuse to visit a bookstore. A library harbors the past. The bookstore tells me what's on people's minds this week. I don't know any place where time passes more quickly for me. I seldom leave without a parcel in hand. "Alas, where is human nature so weak as in the book store!" sighed Henry Ward Beecher.

My wife buys everything from books to shoes to end tables from catalogs and the web. What a waste!

I want to go to a store, where I can see and feel the goods. And what website offers try-ons, answer me that? I also get to speak with real people, known as salespersons. For my money, "web shopping" is an oxymoron.

My youngest son actually reads books on a hand-held gizmo. Appalling! Perhaps acceptable for a science fiction thriller, but can you imagine communing with an electronic Raskolnikov or Emma Bovary?

All right, I confess that I do listen to recorded books when in my car. But only of the sort that Graham Greene called "entertainments"—Le Carré, P.D. James, Greene's own *Confidential Agent* or *Third Man*. The sacred canon of classics and the current with literary pretensions must be imbibed by the eye, not distracted by traffic lights, police sirens, left turns and the need to stop to pick up the dry cleaning. You can lose yourself in a book. You'd better not lose yourself when behind the wheel of a killing machine.

For the same reason, I want to see movies in a theatre, not DVD'd in my living room, when the magic is spoiled by a phone call from Aunt Betsy or from yet another sanctimonious but paid hustler for yet another laudable cause.

I know young people who read the morning newspaper at their computer. An intense scrutiny, no doubt, a determined keeping-up. These benighted souls lose the lazy pleasure of spreading the paper out beside a cup of coffee and leisurely traveling the world, with all its horrors, heroes and curiosities. It's easier to leave my bed in the morning knowing this familiar rite awaits me. And there's the crossword, of course, and if you tell me the crossword can be done on the computer, we have nothing more to say to one another.

I am not denigrating the genius of the computer, or suggesting you unplug it and ship it to your seven-year-old granddaughter. I only want to relegate it to its proper sphere, chiefly as superior typewriter and games adversary. I also value E-mail for contacting those who invariably talk a blue streak on the phone. And I grant the Internet its virtues. It's a devilishly clever skinflint in tracking down the cheapest air fares and hotel rooms. I also allow that computer time beats sitting passively in front of a TV screen. At least the mind gets some exercise.

But the machine must be made to know its place. Print comes first. Sneer at me as a hopeless old Luddite, if it pleases you. I really don't care what you think. I've spent a lifetime with newspapers, books, libraries and shops, and I'm not about to throw them over for blogs, whatever they are.

AH FOR THE DAYS
WHEN MEN WERE MEN AND WOMEN WERE GIRLS

●

We men of an earlier generation—make that several generations—have come to terms, however grudgingly, with what women call their liberation. After all, we witnessed the walls come tumbling down, and denial would get us nowhere.

Still, acclimatization has come hard. When we were growing up, women were merely wives, mothers, cooks, cleaners, launderers, decorators, grocery shoppers, sewers, knitters, canners, nurses, chauffeurs, child psychologists, schedulers, domestic peace keepers, and sometime saints.

Our own fondly remembered mothers, living in what now seems an antediluvian age, catered to, and fussed over, their sons (as dad may have done daughters, but dad wasn't around all day), and we looked forward to a pampered continuum in our connubial years. My adolescent concept of marriage came from fiction and film in which the heroine hoped for nothing more in life than Mr. Right, defined as someone with a full head of dark, wavy hair and a steady job. To assuage any doubts that said male, or his acceptable facsimile, may have had about committing himself to matrimonial shackles, she swore that she would make him "the happiest of men."

Perhaps you, too, recall the once-popular syndicated columnist Dr. Crane. I remember his advising girls having trouble snagging a husband to get a job as a waitress. Male customers being handed heaping plates of meat and potatoes by a smiling young woman would inevitably envision a home life of similar subservience and bliss, and proposals were certain to follow.

And that's the way it was, more or less. The man ruled the house, which the "little woman" kept tidy, providing therein for his comfort, which included a hearty breakfast before work and a hearty dinner at homecoming, after which he disappeared into his basement workshop, leaving the wife to wash the dishes and weep over paperback romances. The children were her responsibility, of course. He hardly spoke to them unless they came to him for money, since he controlled what were called, perhaps graphically, the purse strings.

Even ante-Friedan roles were in reverse speed, until now it is expected that the husband's role—nay, duty—is to make the wife the happiest of women. There could be hell to pay should he fail to please. "Yes, dear," defines the male's domestic conversational repertoire. Husbands see that rebellion is futile, counterproductive if there is to be any household peace. So we submit.

Our own wives may well be college educated, perhaps pioneering doctors, lawyers, scientists or other lofty professionals. What I--my notions stiff with age--find particularly difficult to come to terms with are the women who now rule in business— and I don't mean running little antique shops but managing portions of, or entire, corporations. I see these tailored women everywhere. They have clearly abandoned frying pan and stroller for briefcase and cell phone. They strike me as a new gender, a sport, hermaphroditic.

After all, women are the softer sex--in Nature's wisdom, not society's. Our chests, for example, are very different from theirs. But there they are, presiding, commanding, dominating, limo-ed to private jets that whisk them hither and wherever, to stride, Patton-like, past unbelieving blue-collar workers at a plant site or bully security analysts at an investor relations interrogation. Amazing!

Women who head Fortune 500 companies presumably have little time to shop the post-Christmas sales for a new jacket for little Freddy, much less minister to hubby's tiresome winter bout of flu. The house, too, is nursed by outsiders, and take-out and eat-out have replaced cook-in. As for conjugal intimacy, I think of a *New Yorker* cartoon. A lost soul in pajamas and slippers is sitting in an office reception room. The receptionist, phone in hand, informs him, "Your wife will sleep with you now."

In the lower classes, I am led to believe, the old ways still prevail. Girls there still wind up in maternity wards, not colleges. Their monosyllabic truck-driver husbands slap them around the kitchen if the meat loaf is not sufficiently well done. But these are people I know only from screen representations, and what do Hollywood writers and directors know about people who actually sweat for a living?

Where, I worry, will it all lead? I presume that even women of determined ambition still want a husband, if only to produce one-and-a-half children, and have someone on hand to shovel the driveway so they won't miss an 8 AM meeting, shine their Ferragamos, deal with bugs and mousetraps, and flag down taxis in the rain. They may, then, when still single, flirt, flatter and practice the ancient wiles. And how we'll continue to lap it up, even when we suspect nowadays that it is probably just role playing, and that after the "I do" will come the "you do." But courtship ritual, too, may disappear, since the liberationists probably find it degrading to practice seduction. A pity, since the continuation of the human race depends on it.

Look, I know one can't turn the clock back to some age—even before my time--when husbands were lords of the manor and hovel, and wives were items on a chattel inventory. I understand, too, that the liberation of women is also the salvation of men, forcing us into responsible adulthood instead of remaining coddled children. I appreciate, as well, the financial benefits we now enjoy from spousal income. It is lovely to fly business class to Ocho Rios instead of traveling Chevrolet-class to Virginia Beach.

Still, the good old chattel days, at least as imagined, are delicious to dwell upon. While vacuuming the living room, peeling the salad cucumber, or standing in line at Safeway, I daydream, smiling. Slavery has its appeal, provided you are not the slave. Ostensibly enlightened, I am patently, *au fond*, an unregenerate male chauvinist.

>And I'll tell you, ladies, so are we all.

>As if you didn't know it already.

THE WHITE AND THE BLUES

●

"Look outside, dear! Isn't the snow beautiful, the way it highlights every branch and twig?"

Yeah, it's beautiful. And cold and slippery and a pain to clear from the walk and driveway and hazardous to man and car. And soon, icy and slushy and dirty and ugly. Who needs this stuff?

Children do, of course. They love snow. I know because I was a child once. But that was ages ago, and there are no children around the house now. When my sons went off to college, their sleds slid into the fireplace.

No wonder when winter comes we old folks fly south with the birds. Cold is our enemy. It invades our very bones. It shortens our breath. It coarsens our lips and hands, and leaves painful fissures in our fingertips. It goads our arthritis. We can get depressed enough without the help of this blanket of blankness.

Whenever I visit a nursing home, I'm struck by how warm—nay, hot—they keep the place, year-round. And yet I see the residents---"residents" is the designation preferred over "patients" or "the dying"—are wearing heavy wool sweaters.

One has to wonder if hell wouldn't be our venue of choice.

I, too, would join the elderly refugees beating it for Phoenix, but the desert is such in more ways than the sand and cactus. Winter in the East means concerts and plays and special exhibitions, and I'm not ready to trade them in for bluegrass, a touring Grand Ole Opry and a showing of Frederic Remington cowboys. So I'm a stay-at-home, mostly hibernating indoors, with the thermostat at about 72°, and let the energy conservationists be damned. Any time the snow on our premises is too deep for me to dispel with a broom, I pay someone an exorbitant sum to remove it. When venturing out to the supermarket or barbershop is unavoidable, I do what my mother always advised: bundle up. I wear flannel shirts, flannel-lined pants, husky sweaters, padded parkas, stocking caps pulled down over my ears, wool-lined gloves, thick scarves and heavy boots. I waddle through the drifts with clenched jaws, cursing the oh-so-beautiful snow.

Neolithic man said it right: "Heat good, cold bad."

My wife, my junior by a good many years, still suffers at night from what are called hot flashes, which I, like most males, always assumed were momentary blips. But she's discomfited much of the night and finds an arctic temperature in the bedroom ameliorative. As I explain elsewhere, I moved down the hall several years ago, but my own bedroom is on the same thermostat. I augment the furnace's muted output with an electric heater and an extra blanket or two. I've suggested that my wife might be more comfortable sleeping out back, and have offered to buy her a tent from L.L. Bean. Then I'd have the thermostat to myself.

Several vacations ago my wife and I sweated our way through four 100° days of surveying ancient ruins in some far-off country. At the airport, waiting to depart, I suddenly exclaimed, "M'god, my back!"

"What's the matter?" my wife asked, only somewhat alarmed, given the regularity of such expostulations from her spouse. "I told you to let a porter handle that suitcase."

"No, no, it's not pain. It's the *absence* of pain. My back feels just fine for the first time since I don't remember when."

My euphoria didn't survive the long flight home, but I pondered the respite from the spinal demons and decided that it was the heat that had performed the miracle. As soon as we had settled in at home I went looking for a sauna to install in our basement or master bath or smack in the center of our living room, if necessary. I would create my own tropics and sweat out all my aches and pains.

I soon found, however, that a sauna installation would melt the budget, and thought it best to first give my theory a test. As it happened, we soon attended an out-of-town wedding and stayed at a hotel with a sauna. Ah, a laboratory was at hand! After twenty minutes in that dry inferno, I spent equal time in the adjacent steam room.

Sadly, no healing transformation was discernible. My back gave the heat the cold shoulder. Maybe instead of just sitting there fidgeting I needed to replicate the excavation exploration and climb up, down and around the wooden benches in both facilities. In any case, when I mentioned my intended self-prescribed therapy to my doctor, he tut-tutted. "All that heat, old fellow, isn't smart for someone your age. Not good for the heart, I'm afraid. Better cool it." So I cooled it. I now take tepid showers.

Ah, well, winters don't last forever, at least not in my part of the world. I am confident that however provokingly poky the seasons, spring will come again. And then, praise be, the healing power of July and August—though I confess that I am usually still found indoors, with the air-conditioning at 72°.

OH MY ACHING METATARSUS

•

A high-minded protector of the public purse has complained that Medicare's largesse encourages old people to run unnecessarily to their doctors for every little twinge and tickle. He cited with scorn those who hasten to podiatrists whenever their toenails exceed an aesthetic length.

Let that fool (not even sufficiently informed to know that Medicare doesn't cover such parings) live long enough—but no longer—to experience thickened, fungus-toughened toenails that surrender only to the equivalent of garden shears, and the stiffened back that groans in protest when asked to perform the contortions necessary to deal with the stubborn, half-ingrown suckers.

I, for one, like my podiatrist well enough, but have no desire to see him more often than is necessary. I would much rather stand on, and deal with, my own two feet. I bought a heavy-duty nail clipper that I manage—just barely now—to squeeze with sufficient authority to topple slivers of obdurate nail.

As we age we become increasingly foot-sore, all too familiar with corns, calluses, bunions, heel spurs, fallen arches, swelling, tendonitis and distressing conditions with ugly names like plantar fasciitis, Morton's neuroma and metatarsalagia. All these misfortunes hurt like hell. You bet we visit the foot doc. And become suppliants of devices like arch supports, foam insoles, heel cups, and assorted cushions, pads, liners, wedges and shock absorbers. At various times I've swathed my toes in lamb's wool, gloved them in polyethylene, and isolated one from another by intercessory fences of foam. I am sure that you, too, receive catalogs filled with such items. Our feet are the only extremities to support a cottage industry.

One needn't wait years to experience these miseries down below, of course. I've had a corn on one piggy ever since I can remember. I blame its presence on my mother's attempt to stretch the family's Depression budget by stretching the life of my shoes, choosing to ignore her son's propensity to grow, his feet no exception. Infuriated that a little husk on my toe has the gall to threaten my mobility, I have since early youth attacked this ever-resurgent outcropping on my own.

I first bought an innocent-looking but nasty little blade for the purpose, but every time I used it, I was convinced I was giving myself blood poisoning, and nervously drenched the toe in rubbing alcohol both before and after the surgery. Still sensing threat, I began the practice of soaking my foot while doing a crossword and then trying to tear the carapace off with my fingernails, often quite successfully.

Mostly I have relied on dear Dr. Scholl. I apply his little disks drenched in salicylic acid (weren't they once called Zino Pads?), though podiatrist after podiatrist has warned me against them. Why, I ask petulantly, suspecting the good doctors are most worried about loss of income if such a simple and inexpensive home remedy is effective. Because those things will burn a hole in your toe, the doctors have told me. Nonsense. After years of applications, I see no excavation in that toe, and if Dr. Scholl's puissant plasters had been digging burrows in countless toes all these years, the company would have been sued out of existence ages ago and Dr. Scholl himself would have fled to Bavaria, or wherever his ancestors resided.

Along with the foot ailments and sensitivities comes an obsessive quest for comfortable shoes. If we are to go anywhere, our feet must be shod. And for decency's sake, too, for a person's feet are not the most attractive part of the anatomy, and an old person's feet can be downright repulsive. One tries to pillow them in comfort, perhaps even make them cozier than when naked.

Around the house, it's slippers. "Slippers" is surely one of the warmest and friendliest words in our language. They imply relaxation, disqualification from heavy labor, and an unmistakable signal that one is not prepared to deal with the rigors of the outside world. They suggest fireside and good old Bowser. Fleece-lined, if you like, and of some compliant fabric rather than unyielding leather. One hates to take them off, unless it's time for bed, because their dismissal means only one thing—it's time to face the elements and deal with civilization.

Sneakers—or what we once called tennis or gym shoes—are perhaps the best slipper surrogate, unless it be sandals. But both, we are admonished, are not long-term friendly, something to do with our arches needing more substantial propping. Besides, there are so many occasions when sneakers and sandals are inappropriate. They wouldn't do for a White House reception, for example, even in these careless days. Sorry, but one simply must put on shoes.

I remember the happy day when I was introduced to Rockports. Here were shoes that looked law office or Wall Street but underneath, cunningly, imitated tennis shoes. I always felt guilty wearing them though. A pin-striped suit, a French-cuffed shirt, a silk foulard—and, sub rosa, tennis shoes? My feet should be regulation encased in soles and insoles of pitiless leather, and I should be indifferent to any pain incurred thereby. After all, women are routinely foot martyrs to fashion.

But as we grow older, we become if not wiser, less caring. Comfort me with Rockports or their vast progeny, and the hell with propriety.

Of late I've found another name to honor—Mephisto. This company's footwear is engineered and stitched in France. Perhaps German scientists were abducted after World War II and put to work in a shoe laboratory. Whatever their "biomechanical design," I was all smiles the minute the salesperson eased them onto my feet.

Trouble is, Mephistos cost three or four times more than

Rockports. Nevertheless, I bought a pair. I seldom wear them though. For one thing, at these prices, I expect them to last the rest of my life, however much be left of it. And shoes that valuable can hardly serve as ordinary day wear. They must be reserved for special occasions, like my 100th birthday party. So I wear my cheaper shoes, sorrowing for my Mephistos. Have I learned nothing in my eighty years on this earth? I guess I am like my mother. After her death—in her nineties—we found drawers full of the expensive gifts we had given her, obviously, in her estimation, too good to be actually worn.

Eventually, foot problems solve themselves. After the cane and the walker comes the wheelchair, and one's feet slip into retirement. Either that or you hardly ever leave the house anymore, so it's perpetual slipper time.

AUTO MOTIVES

•

The day I turned 75 my wife had a surprise for me. She called me outside, smiled—somewhat enigmatically I remember thinking--then handed me the keys to a resplendent new Jaguar beside her in the driveway.

I went wild with outrage.

"How could you do this to me?" I wailed. "You violate my very soul!" Does she, I expostulated, who knows me so well, really think I am someone who drives around in a Jaguar? I, a man of the people, of humble origin and pretentions, a democrat and a Democrat? (Only in Hollywood are Democrats allowed to drive Jaguars.) I have always snarled at the country-club set in their Jags, BMWs and Mercedes. I would never want to be one of them. I am far too proud.

Now I was the owner of the symbol of a status I had no wish to claim. "Return it . . . instantly!" I cried.

"Can't. It's paid for. You're always saying the Jaguar is the most beautiful car on the road, so I thought you should finally have one. Look, you're seventy-five. This is your last buggy. You can drive it until they put you in a home and take away your keys."

So I was stuck with the thing. I called friends to complain and seek commiseration.

"Wow, you're a lucky man! A car like that! A wife like that!" I heard more or less the same words from all of them. "Drive it and rejoice. You deserve it."

Deserve it? Of course I don't deserve it, another reason acceptance is bitter. I didn't labor for the purchase price; she did. (Never mind what macho resistance that fact was stirring.) Deserve it on some kind of lifetime merit system? Absurd. I've never been a good enough person for gold-star rewards. I feel myself lucky to 'scape whipping.

All religions, all philosophies, decry profligacy and ostentation. "Sell that thou hast and give to the poor," Christ exhorted. "Moderation in all things," wrote Terrence, picking up on

Aristotle. "All anyone needs is transportation, something to get you from here to there." That was spoken by my eldest son. I am proud to have such progeny.

And here I am with heated seats while half the world goes cold in winter. With an electrically-operated sun roof when millions sleep under leaky tin and thatch. The annual insurance tab, I am sure, would feed six Cambodian families for a year.

I have always driven good cars, you understand—a Toyota, a Buick, even a Lincoln. But I bought them used, three or four years old, when they cost no more than a new Ford. That way I could feel both privileged and virtuous at the same time. Now I must simply be one of the privileged. It's intolerable.

It isn't just the car itself, you understand. It's all that a vehicle of such magnificence imposes. I can't drive a Jaguar, for example, in my usual saggy sweater, worn-knee corduroys and dirty sneakers. It has to be Polo. When valet parking is unavoidable, I suppose a five-dollar tip is now expected (an expectation not met). I've wondered if I can continue to do my humble community work. Aside from the embarrassment of driving into a rundown neighborhood in a rich man's car, the vehicle must inevitably arouse envy and ire. I wouldn't blame anyone if I came back to find a stolen sound system (leaving behind its umpteen speakers) or a knife blade's scar along the hood.

I've even wondered if this isn't the first step in a personality transformation, if my new transport environment won't corrupt me entirely. Shame at being seen in such splendor will insidiously evolve into pride. I will begin to look down upon the drivers of mere Hondas and Chevys. I mean, move to Park Avenue and see how readily you forget the benighted who live in wretched tenements fifteen blocks north. You begin to rationalize, congratulate yourself on some heretofore-unrecognized traits that have elevated you above your fellows. This could not be mere chance; it is a wise God's will that I am blessed with a plush coach while others drive carts. I will soon feel like the Marquis de St. Evrémonde in *Tale of Two Cities*, looking out of his carriage on the "vulgar" as if "they had been mere rats come out of their holes."

Even if I am able to resist the pull of patrician superiority, my defensiveness about my good fortune could develop into an apologetic shyness and compensatory aloofness that will surely be taken for snobbery. One way or the other, I have isolated myself from the masses. I will now be shunned as one of the unapproachable elite.

Putting aside such disturbing projections for a moment, I must say that I have found my imperial chariot the smoothest, quietest, easiest-handling, most responsive and all-around satisfying car I've ever owned. It isn't just the label you're paying for, you know. It's quality, and there's a lot to be said for quality. At an early age, from my very own father, I learned that one should, whenever possible, buy the best. It will last longer, give less trouble, pay off in the long run. You wouldn't want to own a drugstore espresso machine, would you? Or a bargain-basement defibrilator? Well, a car is just another appliance, and a damn important one. This Jaguar is reliable, the seats accommodating to my ancient body, the controls safer for my ancient mind. It's just a pity this ease and confidence had to arrive in a snob package, but there it is. Couldn't be helped.

And it is a lovely thing. My wife is right: I've always admired the Jaguar's profile above all others on the highway. A thing of beauty is a joy for Everett. For me, a car is a piece of sculpture that I display on the road and admire and pet in my garage. I know nothing about its intestines. I have no idea, for example, of the meaning of the "variable cam phasing" my new machine boasts that it possesses. I buy on looks, trusting the manufacturer has learned how to make the thing move when spurred.

Whenever I start to wonder if it wouldn't be best to trade the thing in for a Buick, I tell myself that I am an old man. When people see a thirty-year-old drive a car like this, they're put off. Either he or she inherited big money, and is therefore rightly envied and despised, or is in some shady business or predatory profession, like putting together frivolous class action suits. But a driver my age stirs no hostility. People figure the old coot probably drove around in a Dodge all his life and finally tapped the last of his savings to taste the sweetness of luxury before they put him in the ground.

Well, in any case, the deed was done. I knew I would just have to resign myself to bearing my posh burden. My conscience nags me from time to time, but I have proved resolute enough to master it. I remind myself that one can live the good life and still be a good person. But it's been tougher going.

AND REMEMBER, DRIVE CAREFULLY

•

John Updike mourned that with age he suffered from "a doddering deliberation of movement mixed with patches of inattention and uncertainty that makes my car-driving increasingly hazardous and—other younger drivers indicate with gestures and honking—irritating to others."

Ah, yes. Hazardous and irritating to others, and hazardous and humiliating to ourselves.

Nervous about our undeniably diminished powers, we drive far more slowly than when we were young and immortal. We're now the only ones who actually observe the speed limit. We figure that a fumble at full throttle would compound the damage. Those trailing impatiently behind us don't appreciate our grey hairs and humanitarian caution. They pull ahead of us at the first opportunity, favoring us in passing with those callous gestures that Updike and all of us have suffered.

I will say, though, that at times I suspect some older drivers enjoy the frustrations of those in their wake. The slow track is a turn-on, an expression of passive-aggressive tendencies. I'm thinking of the dear soul who put-puts along at 30 miles an hour in a 50-mile-an-hour no-pass zone. She may be timorous, unsteady, peripherally blind and unawares. But I wonder if this hunched-over old girl, however grimly stony-faced, is chuckling to herself over her power to thwart the twenty cars she is dragging behind her.

Our worst nightmare is that senility will triumph, that we will get befuddled enough to have the car in reverse when we thought it was in drive, or hit the accelerator when we meant to brake, and plow our car into another car, a store front, or—too painful to contemplate—a pedestrian. It happens, we know from the newspapers. We reassure ourselves that we are not yet in that parlous stage, but the possibility haunts us.

I've had tremulous intimations of what could happen from little lapses of concentration, momentary inattentions, though I well understand that being behind the wheel of a lethal weapon is no time for wool-gathering. I start to change lanes or make a turn when I think I have the right of way when in fact it's the wrong of way. Another driver's blast pulls me back just in time. That time just in time, but next time?

Even when we're reasonably confident of the command of our own vehicle, we fear the driver personalities of others, particularly young road Hydes—mostly male, though some women exhibit equal ferocity—who have to show other drivers who's the wimp and who's the whip. They stow forbearance toward careful drivers like ourselves in their glove compartments. They sound their horns before the traffic light has quite made it to green, try to pass us even when they have to cross the double-yellow line, and are forever jiggering in and out of traffic, almost brushing a fender as they gun ahead. Let them pass, the barbarian bullies.

The most ancient of us reach a time, as we assure and reassure our concerned kin, when we drive only within the neighborhood for essential errands, sticking to familiar side streets and avoiding the heavily trafficked. We're out in the rain perhaps, but never when it's snowing, for fear of a skid factor beneath our wheels. And we venture out only in the daytime. At night we are like deer: oncoming lights dazzle and confuse. The old eyes can't take it. Besides, at night landmarks are indistinct, the familiar unfamiliar, unfriendly and vaguely threatening. We're early to bed anyway.

I may tremble at times at thoughts of the harm I can cause, but I'm grateful when they renew my license. Little would be more devastating than taking away my ability to drive, leaving me stranded, housebound, dependent and probably despondent. It would be all over, life come to a stop sign.

The only thing worse would be immobility on my own two legs. And that's bound to happen, too, if I'm around long enough. Then I'll be parked and pushed around in a different vehicle.

JUST LOOKING, THANK YOU

●

For escape, solace and renewal, some meditate, some take nature walks, some contemplate the ocean, some sit in silent churches, some frequent spas, some listen to Bach—or recorded bird calls--in a darkened room. Whatever works.

Me, I head for a shopping mall.

I mean it. I can always come up with an excuse for an excursion, even if it's for a birthday card I could buy at the drugstore. A mall is an ideal haven for older people. It is Hemingway's "clean, well-lighted place," updated. Malls are orderly and safe, unlike many of the streets outside. And determinedly cheerful and inviting. After all, management wants its guests in a money-parting mood.

But it can't be any old mall. It must be one of those upscale places with acres of marble, brass balustrades, exotic flora, and a spacious atrium with a pool or fountain. A concierge desk is a nice touch as well, completing the semblance to a Hyatt hotel lobby. Older, rundown, shabby malls are a disgrace to the franchise, no better than mercantile tenements. They offer no more uplift than a supermarket.

The big malls all have an anchor department store or two, which adds a dimension to the mall experience, a change of pace and space. But standalone department stores don't do it for me. Men's furnishings are on first, clothing on fifth, so you traverse realms. But the verticality is confining. The mall, ranch-style, sprawls. You are walking towards a horizon, not escalating. I like that luxurious expansiveness. And not just the merchandise but the purveyors--each shop with its own personality--change every hundred feet.

I'm after tranquility, so I usually avoid weekend and evening visits. I go when most adults are at work and their kids at school or camp. Of the sparse number of pilgrims around me, a good portion are fellow retirees on a similar quest. We exchange nods and feel at home.

Sometimes, though, I attend at the busiest hours, a deliberate jolt from the quiet of my residential sanctuary. Malls are the castles of our day, within whose walls the community gathers. I go to inspect every species of humanity and contemplate twenty-first-century man, *homo consumerus*, in his native habitat.

I might start my outing with a cup of coffee and a cinnamon something. Then I stroll the corridors, the most painless way in the world to get in that mile or two of walking that's invariably prescribed for us old folk. And there are plenty of benches for breath-catching and spine resuscitation.

I'll look in all the windows—probably pausing at a Victoria's Secret longer than is seemly—browse in a bookstore, judge ties and finger sweaters, marvel at the electronic gadgetry. If there's a Brookstone's, I usually pay a call. I consider their shops intriguing galleries of contemporary craft and ingenuity.

What am I shopping for? Nothing, really. I rarely buy anything. We old people have long acquired all that we need. Oh, at times there's a present to buy, or a pair of shoes, and I—unlike most men—enjoy the process of visiting several shops and solemnly comparing choices, pondering when to unsheathe my credit card.

If I need some big-ticket item, like an overcoat, I may

drive to a discount mall. But these jaunts are purely transactional; there's nothing recreational about them. The ambience is different. People are there only to acquire, not to meander and savor without strong purpose. The purity of the true mall experience is lost.

The posher malls have a few expensive emporia, and I wander through them as well, feeling morally superior because I am not in the least tempted by extravagant baubles. I'll pick up a dress shirt, see it costs $150, shake my head with disbelief and disapproval, and before the sales clerk can reach me with obsequious inquiry, return it to the counter, straightening the pile like the good citizen I am.

I usually spend nothing, then, except my time. "Just looking" indeed. But the authority to inspect and reject always gratifies me. It almost qualifies as entertainment.

I often dwell the better part of a day at my mall, sauntering, peering, judging, marveling at the cornucopia of our civilization. I'll have some lunch at the food court and perhaps take in a movie at the adjunct Cineplex. I return home tired and satisfied, feeling as though I have had a refreshing change of environment, a minor adventure in a foreign realm, the equivalent of a mini-vacation.

If and when I reach the age when I am no longer ambulatory, I hope some kind soul will occasionally wheel me along the aisles of a favorite mall. Just to savor memories of kinder days.

WHAT PRICE IGNORANCE?

●

When you and I went to college, sometime during the last century's middle age, daddy could cough up for the tuition without too much grumbling. I attended one of those places with ivy all over the place, and the four-year tab, food and shelter provided, was something like $5,000. These days, the morning newspaper informs me, parents "have seen the cost of an education at a top four-year private college rise to more than $160,000." State universities, for non-residents, are only marginally less confiscatory.

Don't blame it all on inflation either. College tuition increases have left inflation in the dust for years.

My children are long out of college, but what will our grandchildren do? Drop out after high school? Go to college and work at an all-night McDonald's? Have mommy and daddy declare bankruptcy so they can get full-tuition scholarships? Go to college and bankrupt mommy and daddy anyway?

This runaway imposition on those in quest of campus wisdom has to stop, and I know how to do it. Simple, really.

Why do universities keep raising their tuitions? Because, they say, their costs keep going up. Now what do corporations— more pompously known as "the private sector"-- do when costs get out of hand? They take out the hatchets and hew left and right. They call it downsizing.

Well, it's long past time for colleges to downsize.

Have you looked at a college catalog lately? It's as thick as a telephone book. Take a fairly decent school, say Harvard. Here are some of its recent undergraduate course offerings: Fairy Tales and Children's Literature. A History of Zoos. Hip Hop America. Rainforest Conservation. Japan Pop: From Bashô to Banana. Introduction to Investments. The Visual Display of Quantitative Information (something to do with graphs, tables and charts). I Like Ike But I Love Lucy: Women, Popular Culture and the 1950s. Photography as Fact and Fiction. Korean Cultural Identities. Who is a Jew? The Political Theory of Prisons. Columnist

Kathleen Parker reported in the *Washington Post* that at Emory University, "to fulfill a 'History, Society and Culture' requirement, students may choose from about 600 courses, including 'Gynecology in the Ancient World.'"

All amusing ways to kill an hour or two, no doubt, but what have they to do with education? When you and I were hitting the books, they were real books, not this nonsense.

I say, throw out half the courses and fire half the faculty. (Yes, I know about tenure, but, again, do as companies do, and give the redundants early retirement packages or don't replace them when they go to pasture.) By all means, halve the administration, too, while you're at it. Some major bloodletting, with admitted pain, but then a gradual recovery and a healthy body academic. Tuitions will go the other way, and parents can replace their ten-year-old car.

And here's the glorious fringe benefit: Colleges will again start turning out educated young men and women, which, as far as I can see, hasn't been the case for a long time. They aren't acquiring "higher learning" but what Oscar Levant called "a smattering of ignorance."

I am appalled to discover again and again that diplomas

are being passed out to young persons who have never read Plato, Shakespeare (beyond the three plays assigned in high school), Tolstoy or Milton. (Well, at least a few pages of Milton. How much Milton can one take?) Our land is filled with people passing as educated who think the Hanoverian succession must have something to do with Dartmouth's football coaches, who are ignorant of music composed before the Beatles, and who think Giotto is a character on *The Sopranos.* Instead, it seems, they study zoos and prisons and Bashô, whatever that is. In his book on Shakespeare, the crusty critic Harold Bloom trembled that before long college curricula will drop the Bard in favor of "cultural studies" that concentrate on Batman comics and rock music. Sorry, Hal, but it's happened already. Your book is ten years old.

I suppose my fussing about a classical core curriculum marks me as another fusty throwback. A mind in spats. Mortimer Adler's buried and it's time I was, too. Just line my coffin with the fifty-four volumes of *Great Books of the Western World.*

I don't care what you say about me, a university graduate should have had some exposure to the fundaments of knowledge. One can't know it all, of course, unless you're like, well, Harold Bloom. Know-it-alls aren't pleasant to be around anyway. I myself admit to lacunae. A considerable helping of Dante and Proust has been left on my plate, I am behind on my Heidegger, I'm fuzzy on the Han dynasty, I confuse Colbert and Mazarin, every particle of physics is beyond me, my French embarrasses me and all around me when I dare flash it, I've barely dipped into the *Faerie Queene* and have perused only seven of the twelve *Idylls of the King*, I'm not sure who won (or lost, for that matter) the Peloponnesian War, I can't read even Susan Sontag's novels, I've been known to mistake Herzen for Bakunin, I can't keep the Bach family members straight, and I've seen only one W.C. Fields movie.

These are serious lapses, in my own estimation if not yours. Still, I have read a vast passel of books. So has my wife. Our house foundation is cracking from the weight of our accumulation. I take great pride in how much I've forgotten. And I haven't stopped. At present I'm working my way through the last thirteen of Anthony Trollope's forty-seven novels.

What good all this book learning? A troubling question. One can certainly cite many successful men in history who never went to college at all, starting with Al Capone. Leave it to Oscar Wilde, with his Oxford "double first" in the classics and philosophy, to write that "nothing that's worth knowing can be taught."

That's too cynical, even for Wilde. A college education has many practical advantages aside from a higher paycheck. It enables you to feel superior to your parents if they never had one. You'll know stuff to impress whomever you're dating. It definitely helps with crosswords. It makes you feel at home in bookstores on rainy Saturdays. It provides matter with which to occupy the mind when in the barber's' chair or when making love to someone you really don't care for.

So make sure your grandchildren get what was once vaguely known as "a good education." It's available for purchase only at downsized universities.

BUYING TIME, ONE AT A TIME

•

Flipping through a glossy magazine or even surveying my morning newspaper, I am constantly puzzled by the plethora of ads for ransom-priced watches. You know the watches--pardon me, I meant to say "timepieces"—that I mean, the ones turned out by the Old-World aristocracy—Rolex, Patek Philippe, Piaget, Baume & Mercier, Audemar Piguet, Breitling, TAG Huer, Blancpain and their myriad cousins. The runt of their output fetches at least $1,000.

Who buys all these extravagant trinkets? You can get a Timex for $29.95 or a Rolex knockoff from a street vendor for $10 that will, in this Quartz Age, just as reliably remind you that the day is getting away from you. Either vast numbers of the country's wealthy have had their watches serially stolen from their spa lockers or equally vast numbers have decided they simply must have a wardrobe of timepieces, one to match every tie or scarf.

When you and I were growing up, nobody had more than one watch, except the society doyennes who owned a diamond-chip bracelet affair to wear with their ball gowns. What would be the point of a second watch, anyway, when you can wear only one at a time?

Of course, money meant more when you and I were young. Nobody I know, especially in the Depression years, considered installing a Jacuzzi or buying an espresso machine or laying up a store of watches. 'Tis indeed a gussied-up world.

My own first watch was probably a Timex, but upon graduating from high school or some such momentous rite of passage, I was given a Gruen, worn with pride for many years. (Remember Gruen—and Benrus, Elgin, Helbros, Waltham, Wittnauer and Croton, the treasures of our adolescent years?) We had to wind our watches daily back then, of course, adjust the hands every few days, since accuracy was skittish when springs had to do the work, and take them in for a cleaning every eighteen months or so. There's something to be said for technological progress.

Those fortunates who moved ahead in the world would

probably trade up to a "better watch." Mine was a Hamilton, with a 17-jewel movement—no one knew what that meant, but it sounded good--and a gold-filled rather than a gold-plated case. That's the one I expected to serve me for the rest of my days, unless its strap broke as I was leaning over the railing of the Staten Island Ferry.

Watches were like spouses; you were expected to stick with the one you'd chosen. When my father died, I found among his belongings a pocket watch that probably belonged to his father before him. A pocket watch had no practical use for me, so I didn't keep it and have no idea what happened to it. So much for filial respect and ancestral homage.

I have also noticed in the paper that some jewelers offer to take your present watch in trade for a fresh item. Apparently some people now change their watches every five years, just as they do their cars. Or their spouses.

Then there are the watch collectors. There are always collectors. As a boy I collected match books, which, as you remember, were handed out by restaurants and shops as a cheap form of advertisement in the days before cigarettes caused cancer. On shore vacations I would wander up and down the beach gathering discarded match books, to the disgust of my parents, and I must have collected thousands before I destroyed the collection, probably torching it with one of the abandoned matches. Maybe I should have hung on to the lot of them. They might now be worth a great deal of money, as would the comic books my sons kept from earliest childhood if a basement flood hadn't turned them into pulp fiction.

I confess that were I filthy rich, collecting watches would appeal as a hobby. They are, after all, miniature works of art. It must be quite a challenge to come up with something that looks different from the other thousands when your canvas is the size of a silver dollar. It would be too bothersome to wear each of my acquisitions in rotation, so they'd be for display only. Given enough years of accumulation, I'd add a watch gallery to the house, or maybe build a watch cellar next to my wife's wine cellar.

I do own more than one watch, three to be exact. The old Hamilton's around here some place, but my daily wear now is my first quartz, a Seiko, which looks as good as new and keeps time as accurately as any Vacheron Constantin. Then there's my third, my "dress watch," my Sunday and special-occasion best, a gift from my wife. It's ultra-thin, Scandinavian-stark, no numerals on its light grey face, just chaste little dots around the periphery. It is so haughty that it refuses to tell time unless neighbored by gold cuff links. With it on my wrist, I feel a man of position, debonair, poised to tango.

Though I still browse jewelry shop windows, I will buy no more watches. It would be stupid as well as profligate. At our age, one should pare down, not add to a stockpile of inessentials. We kid ourselves if we think our children will treasure the baubles we leave behind, any more than I did my father's pocket watch and stickpin. Our offspring have their own generational tastes and no doubt take pride in the earning capacity to pursue them. These days, apparently, timepieces are the plumes of choice.

EVER THE FOOL

●

We are old, and perforce wise. That's the deal, right, the tradeoff? Whatever we lose through decrepitude, we gain in wisdom. Since the beginning, that's been the premise and the promise.

Yeah, well, I don't know about you, but I have my doubts. I'm wiser, I suppose, but honest-to-Solomon wise? Well, let's just say I haven't overheard anyone around the poker table refer to Mattlin the Sage.

The young aren't likely to gather at my feet to learn the meaning of life. I'm still puzzling about most aspects of that journey myself. The best I could do is toss around the usual clichés, about behaving toward others as our religions admonish and trying to be content with whatever fate hands us. The essayist Joseph Epstein re-stated one of the hoariest of platitudes: "The wise, if they really are wise, know that wisdom begins with the acknowledgment that one knows nothing." He then wisely added, "What the hell good is that?"

A lifetime of experience has taught us all some lessons that to one degree or another have sunk in, thank goodness. We do the same stupid things less often. We're better at smelling trouble, and staying away from it. We're somewhat more likely to keep our mouths shut. We've cooled down, though we still care too much, usually about the wrong things. Would you believe, I occasionally find myself still fretting over an unreturned and irreplaceable book that I loaned to a thoughtless friend fifty years ago.

Speaking of books, I've consumed an appalling number of them in my lifetime, but it is dispiriting how little the lot of them contributes to what could be called wisdom. No wonder so many in the world read only the Bible. It's as good a vade mecum for life's journey as any shelf-ful of volumes, though I would throw in some of the Greek philosophers. Books provide knowledge, but to quote T.S. Eliot—though I have found that on the whole I don't much care for persons who quote T.S. Eliot—"Where is the wisdom we have lost in knowledge?" I think of Kazantzakis' Zorba, who never read a book but instinctively knew what life is for. His life, anyway. I prefer a life somewhat less manic than Zorba's.

Nor have I gained any insights into how the world should be run. Don't come to me for oracular pronouncements about war, poverty, a just polity. My views have been knee-jerk since I was in knee pants. What goes on in the wider world appalls me, but I have no idea where to begin the fixing. All that I have added to over the years is my store of skepticism about the way things are and will most probably remain, and what the hell good is that?

Another prime aspect of life about which I have remained adamantly unwise is women. They are still an alien species that I adore, venerate and, I suspect, fear. I continue to stare at women of all ages and types—not without remnants of carnality, but mostly simply out of wonder and incomprehension. Who are these curious creatures? The Other, most certainly. But then, I had no sisters.

The end of all noble pronouncements about why we're here and what we're meant to learn before we depart is to love one another. Such is the supreme wisdom, however you come by it.

Sublime, and I subscribe wholeheartedly. But boy, is it ever a bitch to put into everyday practice.

Oh, as is regularly pointed out, it's easy to love amorphous "humanity." Stalin's bloodthirsty heart could embrace the proletariat in the abstract. One can even warm toward the casually met stranger. You can smile at and chat with Doris behind the cash register at the supermarket and congratulate yourself on your amiability and adherence to Christ's democracy. Certainly the opposite behavior is inexcusable. To be high-handed with a clerk or waiter is ugly, a symptom of something at the core that needs mending.

But the ability to unconditionally love thy neighbor, or thy sibling or uncle or even parent or spouse, only partially improves with age. At least I've found it so. I'm more tolerant of my fellow man (can there be such a thing as a fellow woman?) than I was when fresh out of college and knew all that there is to know, unlike all the ignorant people around me, but I can't hide from the truth that I am still far too critical, a prejudicial tribunal of one. Susan Sontag said the greatest crime is to be forever judging, and I share her guilt. There is so much to tut-tut about in others, and the temptation to indulge is harder to resist than a morning doughnut. Appearance, intelligence, tastes, opinions, loquacity, sheer boring ordinariness. I accept—well, sort of—that I am not perfect, but one does have standards, and other people seem to fall so disappointingly, lamentably short. Disapproval elbows enveloping love out of the way.

I need a few more years, Lord, to work on this one.

Another expected attainment in life's passage is acceptance of one's self. By now we should have finally figured out who we are and decided it's OK to be that person, no matter the rest of the world's valuation of our sort. You may not, for example, have achieved the once-assumed glory and mansion on the hill. You've proved, in fact, to be more or less a mediocrity, pretty much like everybody else. And that's okay. Honestly. There are more important things in life than fame and fortune, like being happy--which in itself is a bitch of an accomplishment to bring off.

I could tell that to the young gathered around me. But they wouldn't listen. I know I wouldn't have at their age. As psychiatrist Erik Erikson decided, "Lots of old people don't get wise, but you don't get wise unless you age."

DON'T UPSET YOURSELF

●

One of the secrets of living longer, science and sense agree, is avoidance of stress. Yes, of course, excellent advice. There's something of a hitch though: Life *is* stress. You want to avoid stress, die young.

Some people, we're told, are "happy-go-lucky," dodging whatever fate hurls at them or taking it on the chin with a smile. I don't believe it. I can't recall anyone in my experience who fits that description. "Nothing bothers her," you say? Ha! You just don't know. The sentient feel pain. Those who are happy-though-unlucky are a fiction found only in fiction.

Nor have I found that stress melts away as one ages. The trials of adolescence, courtship, career-building and child-raising are behind one, thanks be to heaven, but exasperations continue to follow us around like unwanted strays.

Most of them are of the same ilk that has plagued us through all of life's passages. You bought tickets for the wrong date. Your repaired roof is leaking again. You picked the dumbest mutual fund managers in Morningstar's universe. You just backed into a parked truck. The deer have digested your tulips. Your local package store has stopped carrying your favorite vodka. You just scuffed a brand new pair of shoes. You've left an expensive pair of sunglasses in the rental car. All the usual insults of a callous universe.

And then there are the vexations reserved just for us old folks. I'll skip the stresses of the worn-out body, which torment one so incessantly one gets used to having them around. I'm thinking beyond the corporeal.

Your daughter and son-in-law are living beyond their means. Your grandchildren are being raised as undisciplined barbarians. Your foyer darkens because you daren't get on a ladder to change the bulbs. Medicare doesn't cover your last colonoscopy. You haven't the strength to open a jam jar. Your favorite sweater no longer keeps you warm; nothing does. The chili you love has kept you up all night, and you know it's goodbye chili forever.

The elevator's on the blink and you have to drag yourself up four flights of stairs to the dentist's office. Nobody on the bus offers you a seat when you're dying to sit down. You discover that you left your hearing aids at home. The recycle bin is now too heavy for you to take to the curb. Impatient drivers pass you with contemptuous looks. You have to rush to the bathroom at the critical point in a movie. You can't follow the plot of the mystery you're reading. You have trouble unlocking your own front door.

If you still, at your age, boil up at every minor irritation and disappointment—the major ones are impossible to take with equanimity unless you are the Dalai Lama—you're a fool and you know it. If any wisdom has penetrated while plodding through the years, it should be to realize how little it all matters, especially as the days dwindle down.

My wife is better at handling mishaps than I. Whenever something maddening happens—like the time I collapsed a shelf and shattered five $60 brandy snifters—she calmly declares, "It's not the end of the world." She speaks true. If perchance the end of the world had indeed arrived at that very moment, the goblets wouldn't have really mattered all that much.

Her "not the end of the world" is a powerful statement.

It forces one to stop in one's tracks and consider what is truly important. But after numerous repetitions, its cliché quality bugs the author in me. I need a more exclamatory, pithy, jabbing response to life's sadistic pranks. The mantra I've tried to implant in my brain for many years now is a simple "So what?" A favorite expletive inserted between the "so" and the "what" lends additional, satisfying talismanic power.

Try it out. Imagine your wallet's been stolen, with its just-installed cash and a dozen cards that define and sustain you. Now stop raving at the malevolent gods and say the magic words. So what? Life will go on. What does it matter in the greater scheme of things?

(Please don't ask me to define, precisely, "the greater scheme of things," because I have no better idea than you do what it might be. We don't need to know. There is, there must be, a greater scheme, but I would insist that your wallet has nothing to do with it.)

Other words and phrases have been proposed as ameliora-tory responses to adverse moments. A girl I kissed in high school liked to say, when experiencing unpleasantness (no cause-effect relationship intended), "This, too, shall pass away." Not bad. Sort of like the advice to "be philosophical" when bad things happen to us good people. But "philosophical" is too vague, open to interpretation. People do, after all, have different philosophies, just as they have different religions and tastes in salad dressings. I still vote for "So what?" It is direct. It has punch. It shows defiance, grit, bravura. A thumb in the eye of an ill-tempered Dame Fortune. It gives you Socrates, Aristotle, Aurelius, Kant and Deepak Chopra in one neat capsule.

Don't misunderstand me—I would never suggest that you turn a shrugged shoulder to the sufferings of others, be they in distant lands, on the other side of your driveway or on the other side of your bed. No insensitivity is intended. This mantra is for internal use only.

Nor do I recommend a cavalier attitude towards the remedial. I wouldn't advise a "so what" response to, say, severe chest pains. Get a bypass, this afternoon if possible.

But for all those everyday spilt-milk and goblet-destroying aggravations that can't be wholly averted, we need a reminder that we should take things as they come and not to heart. We elderly must conserve our dwindling energy, not waste it on the irreversible.

So how successful has my handy charm been?

Not very, I am sorry to report.

Oh, I am quite good at offering wise counsel to others suffering the severest calamities, but I've been far less successful coming to terms with the most trivial setbacks of my own. I do believe "so what?" would work if I clung to it, but when something annoying happens, it's gone into hiding. It disappears just when needed, and I spontaneously flare up. Or I remember it too late, after the blood pressure has pole-vaulted and the damage to the system has been done, no doubt chipping a few weeks off my remaining time on the rolls of the living.

On further consideration, I suppose I am at least somewhat better than I used to be in dealing with unwelcome surprises. One does gain some degree of tempering perspective with advancing years. And before those years advance much further, I may not give a damn about anything.

WHICH WAY TO GO

●

Here's a clipping I've kept for years in a file ingeniously marked "clippings."

It seems a titled gentleman from Europe, an expert skier, was trying out a slope in Colorado. As he was nearing the end of his first downhill, workers were hoisting a finishing-line banner for a competition scheduled for later that morning. The hapless visitor slammed into a rope at neck height and his life run was over. He never knew what hit him, or what he had hit. One minute he was thinking—of what? The Rockies versus the Alps? His lunch plans? An investment? Lovemaking that morning? A corn chafing under his ski boot? No matter. It was all over, just like that.

I kept that clipping because it always starts me thinking.

Which is better: a quick death, like the ill-fated sportsman's or, shall we say, a more leisurely one? The man on a downslide had no reason to expect imminent termination, but we oldsters are always looking over our shoulders for the specter in black. I ask myself, since the end can't be very far over the hill now, would I rather be snuffed out by a fatal heart attack or linger with an equally fatal but slow-poke disease, most likely—I hate the very word—cancer? No question that we'd all prefer to die during sleep at the age of 105, but God is seldom that accommodating.

Many would say that the skier's end was exemplary, however premature. No suffering, physical or mental, no drawn-out affair with progressive deterioration, endless treatments and false hopes, and wailing kin in the anteroom. No chance, as literary critic Wayne Booth mused about his own inexorable fate, of the "disgrace" of a death-bed conversion. No fuss and nonsense, no need for goodbyes. Just a hasty departure.

Others are dismayed at the prospect of such an abrupt severance of the self. They want advance notice, time to collect and recollect, sort and reconcile, make seemly farewells, and prepare the soul for its journey. My wife is emphatically of that number. She always leaves everything neat and tidy.

After giving the matter my profoundest consideration, I've decided that offered a choice—which, of course, I won't be--I'd take passage on the long Styx cruise. I do see the advantages of the alternative. A second of surprise and then, *fini*, not even time for panic to set in. A great saving in downtime, pain and angst, not to mention expense.

Instant demise, however, would deprive me of months of high drama. No opportunity to wallow in self-pity, to track my downward spiral with terrible fascination, to agonize over what in my life I might have done differently, to tote up failures and transgressions, to recall with smiling tears the good times and good people, to dig in my memory file to prepare a good-deeds docket just in case the evangelicals are right.. And then to end it all with a show of noble resignation and stoic calm that would win the admiration of all, including myself. Life is a drama, and I could put on a great last act. I'd hate to miss it.

I must insert here the critical qualification that if the grant of an extended leave-taking involves being stricken not into death but into incomprehension and incoherence, the deal is off. The scenario I envisage requires that I have the power to manipulate. If unable to control the stage, I would then hope for death by

Kevorkian.

As for last acts, how about the very final hours, the possibility of the kind of scene portrayed in Victorian novels and their PBS digests? I see myself lying there in bed, blanketed to my chin to spare the assembled the unpleasantness of my emaciation, my piteous head slightly pillow-elevated. The beloved paterfamilias, surrounded by wife, children, children's spouses and the children's children old enough to witness the terrible truth. My eyes would move over the faces of tearful loved ones, bestowing fond farewells and blessings. A touching tableau as the curtain falls.

But no, it wouldn't work out that way. That's not me. I'm sure that lying there weak and helpless and bored with the whole tedious business, I'd be impatient for it all to be over. This is taking too long, damn it. I'd either be irritable—ordering my progeny to stop their mooning and go for a long walk—or attempt some sort of sick wisecracks, ostensibly to ridicule the banal sentimentality of it all, but actually to hide my terror. No, it's better that I take my last gasps while the family is otherwise engaged—perhaps taking a deathwatch break at the local pizza parlor.

There is a special reason for a writer like myself to be enticed by the thought of a drawn-out death: it finally gives one something non-trivial to write about. You could stock a small library with the annals of the doomed. Anatole Broyard, the *New York Times* book reviewer for many years, confessed that "I felt something like relief, even elation, when the doctor told me that I had cancer of the prostate." He got out pad and pen and went right to work, recording relentlessly the fourteen months he had left among the sentient.

Sorry, Anatole, no famous last words or posthumous royalty checks for *Intoxicated By My Illness*. The book didn't make the lists and no studio optioned the film rights. Few readers care to attend the bedside of a dying stranger. Terms like histology, lymphocytes, monoclonal, embolus, ischemia, mycosis, infarction, sarcoma, colostomy and antigens are not reader-friendly. Who wants to listen to lugubrious recitations of hospital stays, hospital releases, hospital readmittances, bad days, good days, relapses into bad days, until finally the writer/patient is too weak to hold the pencil and too far gone to give a damn about a gift to posterity. Do we care that an enfeebled Harold Brodsky dreamed that he bested Michael Jordan at basketball, that John Cheever had a "very gratifying" orgasm (the third-from-last entry in his published journal), or that Edmund Wilson saw *The French Con-*

nection two nights before all connections were severed? No, if granted an extended deadline on my lifeline, I will on no account invite readers to accompany me on my final passage.

Well, whether it's the quick or languid exit is not my decision to make. Either one will just have to do. If in surprise mode, I won't have much opportunity to complain, will I? If I'm slated for the unabridged version, I hope I can manage the business with sufficient aplomb to win the applause of the angels in the far balcony.

A FOND FAREWELL

•

It's time to make my funeral arrangements.

Don't be alarmed, I'm not terminal, nothing like that. It's just that one shouldn't leave such important matters to the last minute or the questionable taste of others, even to those carelessly referred to as "loved ones."

Or are these final arrangements really important? After all, we won't be a conscious witness of the proceedings and can utter no disapproving growl if they botch it all. Why should we care a fig how they hallow our sad remains?

Still, I'm not one to leave things entirely to chance, so I must ponder the scene and its possibilities.

The big, very icky, choice, of course, is between cremation and burial. There's something to be said for each, none of it palatable.

The body's been abandoned by the soul, so get rid of it, burn it, quick and clean and final. That seems efficient, sensible. The thought of total annihilation, especially by a means we've been taught to fear since the age of two, is disquieting, to say the least, but we've been assured that in this instance we won't feel a thing.

With burial, on the other hand, you stick around a bit longer, albeit in a quieter mode. You remain a presence, however aural, and those at the graveside can still feel the emanations. It's your last chance to exert power in a corporeal mode. And the ride to the cemetery in a customized limo is an appealing lagniappe.

There's also the satisfaction of a splendid casket, no expense spared, the envy of those present who can't afford such profligacy. And of an imposing headstone instead of a lowly urn on the mantel. I must think of an inscription for the tablet, something like "Beloved husband and father who never took life seriously enough."

The thought of slow putrefaction, the food-for-worms business, is very off-putting, however. It's sort of ridiculous, too, hanging around like that underground, waiting for nothing but your gradual dissolution, knowing you are evolving toward skeleton-hood, a very ugly state indeed.

I think I'll let economics decide the issue. Cremation, I assume, is cheaper, so cremation it shall be. I've always had an eye for bargains.

Besides, cremation evokes ancient traditions, the funeral pyre, the immolation of heroes, a grieving widow throwing herself on the flames so that death never the twain shall part--though I rather doubt that my widow, a very sensible person, would be so tempted. I'll be satisfied if she flings herself upon my casket—whether destined for flame or sod--her uncontrollable sobs letting all assembled know that though I may not have been the ideal husband, she'll miss my puns and help with the laundry.

There will surely be some sort of farewell ceremony at the funeral home. An officiating prelate will utter the usual incantations. Not being a particularly religious person, at least in any conventional sense, I'd rather dispense with the pieties, but I think proprieties had best be observed for the sake of any believers who show up, family members included. Everyone present is thinking, "This will happen to me, too, one day," and familiar assurances from a vested authority instructed in the mysteries may comfort those pondering their own eventual passage into nothingness.

My children will no doubt say a few words, pretty much the same things they rehearsed at my eightieth birthday party, though the tone will be somewhat more somber. But not entirely. A few warm-hearted chuckles over the foibles of he-who-has-left-us would not be out of order. Filial reminiscences about dad's impossible ineptitude with tools, appliances and computers will evoke knowing smiles. Other comments that provoke smiles I don't want to know about.

I don't think my widow will be able to say anything. Too overcome with grief.

Friends may volunteer memories, though I intend to out-live all my friends.

There must be some music, I suppose. Bach comes first to mind, but Bach seems so pretentious, worthy only of the more august. Don't they usually play one of the deceased's favorites? But Billy Joel's "Piano Man" seems somewhat out of place.

I must also consult my anthologies for an appropri-ate reading, a touch of literate sentiment. Something from Sir

Thomas Browne perhaps, or Donne, Herbert, Crashaw, Young or another of the lugubrious metaphysicals. On second thought, I'll look for a passage that injects a bit of irreverence into the proceedings, to wake people up and remind them that I was a jolly mocker till the end. Thus far, however, I've found no passage that suits. Even my favorite wits—Twain, Wilde, Shaw—turn grave at the prospect of the grave. Twain, in one of his sourest moods, grumbled that "pity is for the living, envy is for the dead."

I hardly expect the envy of the assembled, but I don't want lamentation either. Surely grief must be muffled for one who had lived more than enough years and had reached the time when he had little to offer but a vacuous half grin.

After the eulogies would come a libation. I know my wife will pick a good wine. She always chooses the wine at restaurants. If still sentient, I think I'd be in need of stronger drink. With maybe a beer chaser. One's throat is always dry after a tedious ceremony.

If little sandwiches are plattered around, please, in memory of my favorite, make them pastrami on rye. Hold the mayo, light on the mustard.

At recent funerals I've attended, bulletin boards have been

placed around the room, to which are pinned photographs of the deceased at various stages of his or her life. I suppose pictures of myself as a toddler can be found, but "What a cute baby" seems to me an irrelevant, if not inane, observation to make at the observance of one's demise. Most of my adult pictures were taken during travels—me at Blenheim, at Fontainbleau, at the Palazzo Vecchio, and midst the ruins of assorted ancient Blenheims, Fontainbleaus and palazzi. An utterly boring travelogue. So let's skip the pics, shall we? Let all remember me as I was in full flower, a man of infinite jest and finite sense.

And by the way, I don't want flowers all over the place. I have no particular fondness for blooms. Even those eighteenth-century still lifes by artists who all seemed to share the first name of Jan make me sneeze. Newspaper notices of my demise should ask that intended flower money be sent instead to the Society for the Amelioration of Indigent Writers.

Funerals, if truth be told, with all their dolorous undertones, are rather pleasant occasions. Family and friends meet who never see each other except on a like wind-up occasion. But after a catch-up hour or two the crowd (I assume I will draw a crowd) will of necessity disperse. It will be time for everyone to go about their more important business and leave me to my everlasting peace.

AND AFTERWARDS?

●

If you'll please take a seat, ladies and gentlemen, there's an urgent topic I'd like to discuss with you today. Rather a dreary one, I'm afraid: "Is there really a heaven and a hell hereafter?" Or at least recognizable facsimiles thereof.

Don't give me that roll of the eyes. At our time of life, one must—not after a heavy meal, of course--confront this question, however unpalatable. I understand what a daunting subject it is. We will barely scratch the surface in the time allotted, so no need to take notes.

Whatever one's personal nighttime sweats at the possibility of a flinty judge awaiting us at life's advancing terminus, one can't help wishing for reward and retribution for those egregiously cheated or let off the hook on earth. We hope the decent among us who have had a rotten time of it get to cash in when it's all over, and we can't abide the thought that the nastiest of our lot could get off scot-free. It outrages all sense of fairness that the vicious, too, should go through the tunnel and emerge into embracing radiance. "They behaved badly, yes, but they meant well, and over here we understand and forgive." Uh-uh. *Caritas* can go too far.

Even tyrants well below the Sadam Hussein class--the domestic variety--should pay for their lifetime of careless abuse. In the first episode of "Six Feet Under" a sweet-looking old man looks into the open coffin of his sweet-looking late wife and mumbles, "If there's any justice in the universe, she's shoveling shit in hell." Exactly. Justice in the universe is what we have a right to expect. We want the good guys to get gold stars and a generous eternal pension and the bad guys to suffer a commensurate comeuppance.

But what about you and me--if I may presume to speak for all of us present—who fall somewhere in the middle of the devil-saint spectrum? What must we expect?

Three-quarters of our fellow Americans say they believe in hell. But what percentage of us think we'll wind up there, eh?

Very, very few, I'll bet. And not because we have abstained from serial killing and National Park littering, but because we excuse ourselves for our many peccadilloes, and conveniently overlook the sins of omission, the good things we could have done if only the days weren't so short. In any case, the nature and nurture that molded us were beyond our control. "Hey, I know I wasn't perfect, but I did the best I could, given who I was. You can't be serious about this eternal toasting business."

We also can't believe that the God we've been told so often is a loving and forgiving father would treat us--his creations, his children--so meanly. As the philosopher Lin Yutang reassured himself, "If God loves me only half as much as my mother does, He will not send me to hell." Okay, deliver the equivalent of a spanking, and then let us go off to play. That hell place is for the real bullies on the playground, not us innocuous naughties.

Christian Fundamentalists have no such equivocations. Hell is a very real and well-populated domain. William Buckley told of author Ralph de Toledano's insisting his editor capitalize all references to hell in his book, "because it's a place, you know, like Scarsdale." Its entertainments won't be far off from the depictions of Hieronymus Bosch, Jonathan Edwards and Father

Arnall in *Portrait of the Artist as a Young Man.*

Of course, the devout can be smug about the whole business, because they know Jesus' sacrifice saved them from the fiery pit. When the Jewish reporter Jeffrey Goldberg went to Dallas to interview James Sibley, the Southern Baptist Convention's "missionary to the Jews," the two had lunch at a Tex-Mex restaurant near Sibley's church. Goldberg asked what would happen to him if he didn't convert. "Then you are separated from God," Sibley replied. "Hell?" Goldberg inquired. "Hell," Sibley answered. "Try the chicken burrito. It's excellent."

Heaven, it seems, is a restricted community. Which doesn't seem quite cricket. After all, Mr. Goldberg may be a veritable saint, though that is hard to believe of someone who chose the profession of journalism.

Freud, whom Mr. Sibley believes is suffering eternal torment for failing to embrace the cross, boasted that he had no fears of the wrath of the Almighty. "If we were ever to meet, I should have more reproaches to make to Him than He could to me." Considering all the world's miseries, inflicted on the innocent as well as the malicious, Freud has a valid point in my opinion, but you know who has the upper hand up there.

On occasion, apprehensive about what may lie in wait on the other side, I draw up a balance sheet that would suggest the probable disposition of my own tarnished soul should posthumous judgment be as Biblically advertised.

It is not a very reassuring document.

On the liability side, I've been self-centered, vain, judgmental, petty, arrogant, insensitive, often infantile, hardly a paragon as son, husband or father. In short, I've been the average male. Ask any woman.

On the asset side, I've had to do some real memory digging. The good deeds are not that abundant. As a Boy Scout, I lent my strong young arm to the ancient doddering survivors of the Civil War at their annual powwow, almost their last, held that year in my hometown, Columbus, Ohio. In college, I kindly squired a fellow freshman from the backwoods of Kentucky who wanted a jacket and hat for the coming winter and feared the unknown terrors of a subway and escalators. (He reciprocated by helping me in an unavoidable biology lab; he was used to doing things to frogs.)

In adulthood, I've helped the occasional blind man cross the street and old lady manage a satchel. I've returned borrowed books. I've put quarters in the hands of beggars and once gave a dollar to a sidewalk advocate for threatened whales, though I suspected, as has Joe Queenan, "that not all whales deserve to be saved."

But all that isn't going to get me very far in pleading my case before the supernal bench. My claims to occasional good turns and scattered hours of community service don't add up to much when compared to those who have nursed AIDS patients in Zimbabwe.

But wait! If sins of omission are to be tallied, so should virtues of omission. I register better on this meter. I haven't littered, spit on sidewalks or scrawled graffiti. I haven't lied to the IRS. Nor coveted my neighbor's wife. (If you saw her, you'd know why. Her daughter is another matter.) I've never struck my own wife. (If I did, she would have belted me to the floor before walking out.) I've abstained from racial and ethnic epithets, though I think them when seeing tattooed rednecks buying six-packs in the deli that stocks my favorite cheeses.

I don't recall ever being guilty of sexual harassment either. To the best of my memory, and hard as it is to believe, I've never fondled the occasional buttock preoccupied at a water fountain or rubbed against an angora sweater in an elevator. I am almost ashamed to admit it. You'll think me a wimp, testosterone deficient. But I trust my frailty will be viewed differently on the far side.

But these are piddling matters. What's important, and what I will submit as prime evidence for the defense, are the big, really important omissions. I have not murdered, I have not tortured, I have not molested minors, I have thrown no bombs into crowded cafes, I have not raped or pillaged, I have not been a hit-and-run driver, I have not committed grand (or petty) larceny, I have not taken part in a gang-bashing of gays or Blacks or any other hapless minority.

We all know there are plenty of people out there who have done these terrible things. How truncated our newspapers and newscasts would be without them. These monsters are the ones to shuffle off to hell, not we heirs of Henry James heavy with guilt over some insensitive remark to a friend after too much sherry.

No, I expect run-of-the-mill sinners like me—and you as well, to again presume—will be remanded to some correction or rehabilitation facility, someplace where the beds are hard, the food intolerable and the daily calisthenics last two-and-a-half hours, but none of that pitchfork and flames stuff. There in my narrow cell I can reflect on the folly of the years I wasted on earth and vow to do better next time.

That's the way I see it, anyway. That's what I'm counting on. That's how I comfort myself when foreboding sets in.

But enough. I refuse to deal with this unpleasant business any more today.

Class dismissed.

COOL IT, OLD BOY

•

Do not go gentle into that good night,

Old age should burn and rave at close of day.

What rubbish.

Why, in the name of all that's sane, shouldn't we go gently? What avails burning and raving, puffed up with impotent bravado? There's no escaping "nature's strict economy," as a dying William Trevor character decides. Much cannier to accept, with as much philosophy as one can muster. Or religion, if you have that. By all and every means, gentle yourself, ease off, as you do when it's time to get off the treadmill. Shaking a fist at the heavens may offer a feel-good moment, but the heavens' indifference only leaves you deflated and bitter. Much better to cave in. Besides, being carried off screaming is such bad form, not that

Dylan Thomas was ever troubled by decorum.

Since religion's promises have left me unconvinced, I have consulted the scriptures of the ancient philosophers. They back me up. There's no point in ranting at the Reaper. You know he's going to have his way, so accept with as good a grace as you can manage.

Listen to Cicero: "O wretched indeed is that old man who has not learned in the course of his long life that death should be held of no account." He and Marcus Aurelius came up with the same metaphor: you've made a voyage, you've come to shore, it's time to get out. One thinks of Socrates' sang-froid as he drank from the flagon with the dragon.

I particularly admire the patrician leave-taking of Epictetus: "I must die, must I? If at once, then I am dying. If soon, I dine now, as it is time for dinner, and afterwards, when the time comes, I will die. And die how? As befits one who gives back what is not his own."

That's it, that's the way I must learn to think! Those Greek and Roman greybeards deserve their reputations. They talk sense, ducking the metaphysics. "Philosophy hasn't the egotism of faith," as the nineteenth-century agnostic Robert Ingersoll shrewdly noted. When the time comes, I'll channel Epictetus' noble shade for guidance.

If you really think about it a good long time, dying shouldn't be such a bad thing. Maybe the dying part, but not death itself. At last, some peace and quiet around here. It's like the Dane said, fortune can finally lay off with its slings and arrows.

Our bodies, these latter days, are the recipients of a considerable arsenal of those slings and arrows. The time comes to call it quits to the patching and repairs. You know the proper fate of worn-out things. And what do we say to the newly bereaved? "It was really a blessing. She won't have to suffer any longer." I wouldn't mind losing out on the suffering.

Personally, I am especially looking forward to no longer being a servant to my teeth--of which I still have most, though a few wandered off somewhere along the way. Visits to my dentist invariably lead to further, endless appointments. He always finds reasons for further fiddling in there. A few days before he died, Chief Justice William Rehnquist was asked by an emergency room attendant to name his primary care physician. "My dentist," Rehnquist answered, maintaining his humor and honesty till the end. What a blessing to have no more brushing, flossing, Stim-u-denting, cleaning, scraping, drilling, patching, capping, bridging, root canalling, and periodontists who offer a preview of what the devil has in store. Let that orifice—let all orifices--be shut until further notice.

It's the picayune, day-to-day matters that I smile to leave behind. The big troubles and traumas are probably behind us already—the disappointments, the bungles, the regrets over "the good not done, the love not given, time torn off unused," as the poet Philip Larkin lamented. They now seem part of a drama—with a decent share of comic relief--whose curtain is falling, however much one stupidly dwells upon past scenes.

But the daily list of petty things-to-do and things-to-bear remains, and it would be a pleasure to shred them all. Like the simple household chores—making the bed, watering the plants, laundering the towels, filling the bird feeder, making meals, cleaning up messes, and all the incessant bringing in and taking out necessary to maintain life and stave off chaos. Then come the outside chores. Waiting in line twenty minutes at the post office to see if a letter needs extra postage. Getting one's hair cut and car washed and prescriptions filled. Attending funerals of people you never really liked. Visiting relatives, ditto. Picking out gifts without a clue. Writing little notes on Christmas cards to people you haven't seen in twenty years. Make up your own list of the tedious trivia that is life, and think of the satisfaction of dumping it all for someone else to do and endure.

But why, you object, dwell on the irritations and annoyances when there are still so many pleasures to enjoy? Yeah? Name six. So many of one's once-favorite foods are now forbidden, and, truth be told, the appetite is blunted, even for them. Bland suits best now, and bland is blah. Travel? Nice to contemplate, but in reality the most enticing place on the whole earth is one's own bed. The arts? Yes, there are still books. And music, man's profoundest invention. But as for the theater, opera, ballet and concerts, one has an option at my time of life: doze off during the first half of the program and make out the rest as best one can, or stay awake in the first half and be in a stupor the second. On my increasingly rare visits to a museum, the most captivating artifact is a bench to sit on.

Friends? Lunches and dinners with the few still alive are frustrating affairs. We've known each other so long, and heard each other's opinions on all matters under the sun so often, that after an initial genuine pleasure in seeing a familiar smile, silences ensue, followed by surreptitious glances at the wrist and recourse to another roll.

But your grandchildren—surely you want to see how their lives play out. I'm not entirely certain. I love them the way they are now, sweet and ingenuous. There's too much risk of disappointment down the line.

And my wife, my best friend these many decades, the one who's kept me reasonably sane? Saying farewell will be a terrible moment, but she and I understand that a departure is inevitable, whoever makes the first move.

I'll tell you what I myself most look forward to about death: the shutting off of the buzz in the head, the final damming of the stream of consciousness. I've tried to block the incessant, repetitious chatter with devices like meditation, but it's no use. The mind has a mind of its own. As John Updike has told us, "the electricity in your brain just crackles and crackles until you're dead." Okay, then, pull the plug.

I'm not trying to depress you. I want you to consider the positive side of the inevitable. Yes, life is a wonderful gift, but it comes with an expiration date, and that's a good thing, as Gulliver learned in Luggnagg. I'm past eighty, and eighty years is a very long stretch. Look how much dreary history you and I have witnessed. Forgoing the morning paper, with its fresh atrocities, is another plus in favor of closure.

I was born two years before Anne Frank, in the year Lindburgh flew the Atlantic, so I can hardly ignore the terrain I've finally stumbled into. Death at an early age is tragic, but in the "old age" Thomas is grumbling about, one should submit humbly to the final beckoning, even with gratitude.

Thus I prime myself, whispering encouragement and ancient wisdoms. When time has truly run out, I hope I will be in pacific readiness.

Not that there's any hurry, you understand.